FOOTPATHS OF BRITAIN
WALES

This is a Parragon Book
First published in 2003

Parragon
Queen Street House
4 Queen Street
Bath BA1 1HE
United Kingdom

Created and produced by
The Bridgewater Book Company Ltd,
Lewes, East Sussex

ISBN: 1-40540-508-2

Printed in China

www.walkingworld.com

Visit the Walkingworld website at
www.walkingworld.com

All the walks in this book are available in more
detailed form on the Walkingworld website.
The route instructions have photographs at key
decision points to help you to navigate, and
each walk comes with an Ordnance Survey®
map. Simply print them out on A4 paper
and you are ready to go! A modest annual
subscription gives you access to over 1,400
walks, all in this easy-to-follow format. If you
wish, you can purchase individual walks for a
small fee.

Next to every walk in this book you will see
a Walk ID. You can enter this ID number on
Walkingworld's 'Find a Walk' page and you will
be taken straight to the details of that walk.

CONTENTS

Introduction

Britain is a fabulous place to walk. We are blessed with a varied and beautiful landscape, a dense network of public footpaths and places of historical interest at every corner. Add to all this the many thousands of well-placed pubs, tea shops and visitor attractions, and it's easy to see why walking is a treasured pastime for millions of people.

Walking is the perfect way to keep fit and healthy. It is good for your heart, muscles and body generally, without making the extreme demands of many sports. For most walkers, however, the health benefits are secondary. We walk for the sheer pleasure of it – being able to breathe in the fresh air, enjoy the company of our friends and 'get away from it all'.

Equipment

If you take up walking as a hobby, it is quite possible to spend a fortune on specialist outdoor kit. But you really don't need to. Just invest in a few inexpensive basics and you'll be ready to enjoy any of the walks in this book.

For footwear, boots are definitely best as they provide you with ankle support and protection from the inevitable mud, nettles and puddles. A light-weight pair should be fine if you have no intention of venturing up big hills or over rugged terrain. If you are not sure what to get, go to a specialist shop and ask for advice. Above all, choose boots that fit well and are comfortable.

Take clothing to deal with any weather that you may encounter. Allow for the 'wind-chill' factor – if your clothes get wet you will feel this cooling effect even more. Carry a small rucksack with a spare top, a hat and waterproofs, just in case. The key is being able to put on and take off layers of clothing at will and so keep an even, comfortable temperature throughout the day.

It's a good idea to carry some food and drink. Walking is exercise and you need to replace the fluid you lose through perspiration. Take a bottle of soft drink or water, and sip it regularly rather than downing it in one go. The occasional chocolate bar, sandwich or biscuit can work wonders when energy levels are flagging.

Walking poles – the modern version of the walking stick – are worth considering. They help you to balance and allow your arms to take some of the strain when going uphill. They also lessen the impact on your knees on downhill slopes. Don't be fooled into thinking that poles are just for the older walker – they are popular with trekkers and mountaineers of all ages.

Finding your way

Most walkers use Ordnance Survey® maps, rightly considered to be among the most accurate, up-to-date and 'walker-friendly' in the world. The 1:50,000 scale Landranger series has long been a favourite of outdoor enthusiasts. Almost all areas of Britain are also covered by the more detailed 1:25,000 scale Explorer and Explorer OL series. These include features such as field boundaries, farm buildings and small streams.

Having a map and compass – and learning how to use them – is vital to being safe in the countryside. Compass and map skills come with practice – there is no substitute for taking them out and having a go. Buy a compass with a transparent base plate and rotating dial; you will find this type in any outdoor shop. Most come with simple instructions – if not, ask in the shop for a guide.

If this all sounds a bit serious, I urge you not to worry too much about getting lost. We have all done it – some of us more often than we care to admit! You are unlikely to come to much harm unless you are on a featureless hilltop or out in very poor weather. If you want to build up your confidence, start with shorter routes through farmland or along the coastline and allow yourself plenty of time.

There are plenty of walks in this book that are perfect for the beginner. You can make navigating even easier by downloading the routes in this book from Walkingworld's website: www.walkingworld.com. These detailed walk instructions feature a photograph at each major decision point, to help you confirm your position and see where to go next.

Another alternative is to join a local walking group

key to maps

✆	Telephone	⚲	Lighthouse
●	Start of route		Camping
	Viewpoint	▲	Youth hostel
△	Pylon	⌐	Bridge
	Triangulation point		Windmill
☖	Radio mast		Highest point/summit
♦	Church with Steeple	PH	Public house
+	Church without Steeple	PC	Public convenience
♦	Chapel	1666	Place of historical interest
⚡	Power	⋯	Embankment/cutting
⚑	Golf course		Rocky area/ sharp drop
	Picnic area	▪	Building
	Car park	▪	Castle
	Information	☆	Tumulus
		⁖	Garden

Marsh   Lake/sea

Railway + station

Dismantled railway   Woods

Route of walk   Sand

A Road

B Road   Dunes

Footpath   Urban

Track/unclassified road

Stream

River

Large river/estuary

0   1 km   1 mile

Difficulty Rating   **Time**

Gentle Stroll   Moderate Walk   Each circle = 1 hour

Easy Walk   Hill Scramble   Half circle = ½ hour

and learn from others. There are hundreds of such groups around the country, with members keen to share their experience and skills.

Enough words. Take the walks in this book as your inspiration. Grab your map and compass, and put on your boots. It's time to go out and walk!

Have fun.

DAVID STEWART *Walkingworld*

▲ Map: Explorer 255 or 256
▲ Distance: 10.6 km/6½ miles
▲ Walk ID: 312 Jim Grindle

Difficulty rating
!!!

Time
● ● ● ● ●

▲ Hills or Fells, River, Pub, Toilets, Museum, Castle, Stately Home, Birds, Flowers, Great Views

Llangollen Canal Walk

A walk along the canal with a return by bridleway, which snakes round the hillside offering outstanding views. The walk includes a climb to the top of Dinas Bran, the ancient castle overlooking the town of LLangollen.

❶ Turn right from the car park entrance and walk to the main street. Turn left. Cross the bridge and go half-left across the main road to a passageway with a signpost for canal boats. Go up the narrow path or steps. On the towpath turn right and go under the road bridge. Follow the towpath for 2 km to reach another bridge.

❷ Cross the stile by the gate and turn left on the lane, crossing the canal bridge. Go uphill until you reach Llandyn Hall. On the left is a stile. Go over and up to another stile by a gate 200 m away. Cross the two stiles near to each other. Go half-left across the field. Go through the gate and follow the hedge and then the buildings on the left until you reach a stile onto a lane. Turn right. You will reach a kissing gate and signpost for the castle.

❸ Follow the signpost pointing left. Go over the stile at the end of the path and turn left. Go straight uphill to the castle. On the far side you will be able to pick up a broad, fenced track leading down. Turn right at the second tree. Continue until you reach a fence. Turn left and go down towards a stile. Cross the field to the far right corner to a stile by a lane.

❹ Turn right and stay on the lane for 500 m. Turn right at the junction and look for the signpost for Brynhyfryd.

Turn left and pass a building close on your left and two others up to the right. Go through a gate and onto a grassy track for 1.2 km after which it drops and joins another. Turn left so that you double back. In 120 m you come to a ladder stile on the right. Cross and look for another one in the corner. Go over and follow the field edge.

❺ Follow the sign towards Llangollen. You soon come to a gate. Follow an enclosed track to a road. Turn right. You come to a canal bridge on the left.

❻ Cross the bridge, turn left and follow the towpath for 2 km back to Llangollen.

access information

Llangollen is just off the A5 and is signposted from the A483. There is a car park in the centre of town, again well signposted. There are regular buses to Chester, Chirk, Wrexham and Oswestry.

The Offa's Dyke Path, which runs along the hills above Llangollen, traces the border built between England and Wales in 770, when Wales effectively became a separate Celtic nation.

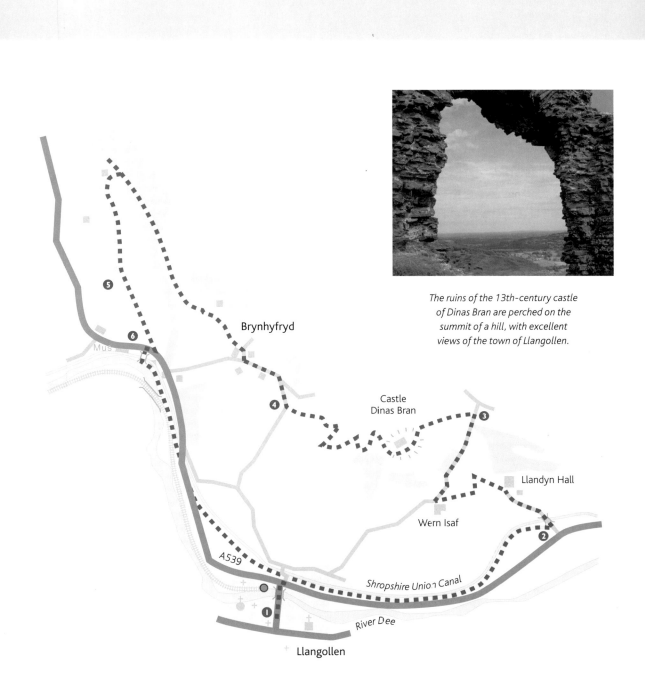

Brynhyfryd

Castle
Dinas Bran

Llandyn Hall

Wern Isaf

A539

Shropshire Union Canal

River Dee

Llangollen

The ruins of the 13th-century castle of Dinas Bran are perched on the summit of a hill, with excellent views of the town of Llangollen.

0   1 km   1 mile

▲ Map: Explorer 256 & 257
▲ Distance: 10 km/6¼ miles
▲ Walk ID: 139 Jim Grindle

Difficulty rating

Time

● ● ●

▲ River, Pub, Toilets, Wildlife, Flowers,
Great Views

Erbistock from Overton

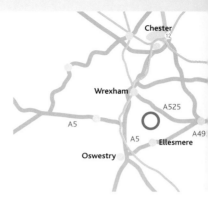

The 'Overton Yew Trees' walk follows the River Dee. The route then climbs and the views are spectacular. A further riverside walk is followed by a second climb to the village.

1 Go through the gate into the churchyard at Overton, with its famous 12th-century yew trees. Cross the road and turn left, passing the war memorial, and walk as far as the sharp bend left.

2 Turn right at the signpost for Maelor Way. Follow the road down the hill to where it curves right. The track goes into the field and makes a dog-leg onto the embankment. Follow this track to the river bank.

3 Turn left at a signpost and keep to the right of the field. The River Dee runs just behind the trees. A footbridge leads to a narrow path through the woods parallel to the river. Leave by another bridge and a stile into a small field. Keep to the right edge and make for the corner. Cross the stile and continue until you are opposite an inn on the far bank of the river.

4 Turn left, up the embankment, via some steps to a stile at the top. Turn left at the stile and then right to follow the line of some fencing uphill to another stile. This stile leads to some steps. Turn left and soon you will cross a stile by a cattle grid. Cross another stile on the left further on into a field. Follow the line of the hedge on the left to a signpost. This directs you half-right round two lines of trees. You must come back left again to a stile almost in the bottom left corner of the field.

5 Beyond the next stile is a path

The River Dee, with its rocky bed, swirls and eddies, and tree-lined banks, flows through peaceful villages and areas of unspoilt natural beauty.

access information

Overton is most easily reached from the A483 (Wrexham bypass). Turn onto the A539 (signposted Ruabon and then Erbistock). Continue on the A539 at the junction with the A528. There is a car park at the back of the church. The main street is wide and has ample parking.

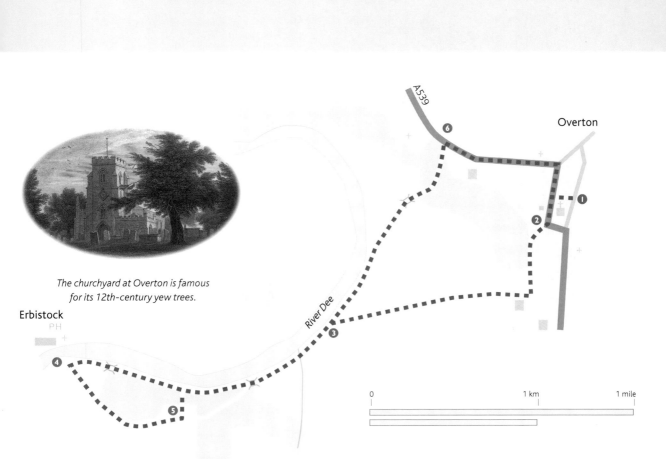

The churchyard at Overton is famous for its 12th-century yew trees.

leading back to the riverside path. Turn right and follow your outward route. At the point where you joined the river, continue alongside the river on the left of the field until you come to a wire fence and a stile. Cross and turn right. Follow the line of the fence as it turns left and then sharp right. Look out ahead of you for a signpost by a gate and a bridge. The path beyond the bridge curves left and uphill. The path ends at the main road, the A539.

6 Cross to the pavement on the far side of the road and turn right for the centre of Overton, back to your starting point.

▲ Map: Explorer 256
▲ Distance: 6.5 km/4 miles
▲ Walk ID: 226 Jim Grindle

Difficulty rating

Time

▲ River, Sculpture Trail, Ancient Monument, Woodland

A55   Chester 12

Wrexham   A534
A483   A525

A5

Alyn Waters from Gresford Bells

The walk begins and ends in Alyn Waters Country Park near Gresford Bells. The park has been created from the site of a large opencast mine and has a sculpture trail. Gradually it moves into tranquil fields by the River Alyn.

1 From the gate at the lower end of the car park follow the path until you reach a silver sculpture. Take the right fork. When you reach a gateway on a lane, turn left. You will see a fork in the road. Take the right fork, downhill. The lane crosses the River Alyn and climbs again.
2 At a sharp left bend go through the kissing gate on the right. Follow the path until you come to a junction with a path. Turn left and follow the path to a gateway. Turn left and go through a car park to the main road. At the road, turn right and continue until you reach the football ground.
3 Go in, keeping near an embankment on the left. Turn left into a gap in the trees and pick up a little path leading down to Sherbourne Avenue. Turn right and in 120 m cross to a signpost. The path passes along the backs of houses to a kissing gate. Go through and turn left. Just after passing the pond on the left the fence takes a sharp turn to the left. Pass a gate with no fence round it to reach a broader track. Turn right here and in 50 m you come to a solitary tree. Turn left by the tree and pick up a path that follows the stream to a kissing gate and a main road. Cross the road to the path on the far side.
4 Turn right into the lane. It goes sharp left after only 20 m to a group of farm buildings. Go between all the buildings

Majestic beech trees and deciduous woodland border the River Alyn, part of the Alyn Waters Country Park.

to the bottom gate. Cross the metal stile and go towards a ruined building. Cross the footbridge over the River Alyn and turn right and follow the river. The route leads past two gates and stiles to a small lane by some houses. Continue to reach a T-junction.
5 Turn left and follow the lane to a crossroads with the B5425. Cross to the lane opposite (Park Road) and walk as far as a sharp left bend, where there is a stile.
6 Cross the stile into Alyn Waters Country Park. There is a narrow green path that you should follow. Cross the broader green path and continue until you come to a tarmac path. Turn right and you will see the car park.

further information

There has been a remarkable transformation of what was once a huge mining area. The latest development, and one which has added an intereting twist to the area, is the creation of a sculpture trail. A few of these witty and entertaining sculptures are passed on this walk, but a wheelchair user could stay in the park and track down many more.

access information

The start of the walk is in the car park of a public golf driving range less than 4 km north-west of Gresford. It is on the west side of the B5425. There are buses from the centre of Wrexham.

Alyn Waters Country Park

B5425

Bryn Alyn

Gwersyllt

0   1 km   1 mile

▲ Map: Explorer OL 17
▲ Distance: 8 km/5 miles
▲ Walk ID: 1419 Jim Grindle

Difficulty rating
👣👣👣

Time
●●●

▲ Hills or Fells, Mountains, River, Toilets, National Trust/NTS, Birds, Food Shop, Tea Shop

Ogwen from Bethesda

From Bethesda the walk descends into the valley and then offers an easy climb up to Ogwen Cottage and Ogwen Falls. An unusual landmark to look out for is a quartz stone by the side of the track.

The rugged, glaciated peaks of Snowdonia form a dramatic backdrop to this walk.

1 Start in the town centre and follow the A5 south. You will go over a river bridge and come to a crossroads on the edge of town. Turn left at the Snowdonia National Park emblem, then right into a street called Rhes James. Go through a gate at the end of this short street.
2 Follow the track and go through another gate. Follow the grass verge through to the woods. The path ends at a stile leading onto open ground. You will find a grassy track that soon turns sharply left. Follow the path. When it fades out, turn right near the remains of a sheepfold into a shallow valley. Make your way up the slope.

3 Follow the higher ground until you see a wall on the right and then follow faint tracks alongside it. One kilometre from here you will cross the first of three streams and go through a gate in the wall leading you into the sheepfold. On the far side of the sheepfold is a stile by a gate – and a yellow arrow.
4 Cross the stile and turn left – there is another signpost on the far side of the wall. Follow the wall to another gate and stile about 100 m away. When you are over this stile look for posts with yellow arrows. They guide you onto a grassy track that leads gently downhill. After 1.5 km watch out for trees surrounding buildings below you on the right. By the track is a quartz stone.
5 The main track continues down to the A5. The right of way doubles back at the quartz stone to a gate in the corner. Go through the gate and follow paths down to the A5. Cross to a fingerpost. Go through onto a path leading to a bridge. The path goes over the bridge, left alongside the low wall and then passes a huge glaciated boulder and a smaller bridge to reach the old road.
6 Turn left and after a climb and 2.5 km you will reach the Youth Hostel at Ogwen. On the main road is Ogwen Cottage and the bus stop.

further information

A few minutes from the end of this walk is Cwm Idwal, a National Nature Reserve noted for its geomorphology and geology as well as for its rare Arctic-alpine plants.

ANGLESEY
Bangor
Caernarfon
Betws-y-Coed
A55 A470
A5
A487

Accessible in any weather, this walk offers outstanding views of a number of Wales' 3,000 peaks.

access information

Bethesda is on the A5 south-east of Bangor.
Buses run from Betws-y-Coed to Bethesda
and Bangor. There are several signposted car
parks in the town. At the end of the walk you
have several choices. You can walk back to
Bethesda or wait for a bus if you are not
being collected here.

Bethesda

A5

Ty Gwyn

Nant Ffrancon

Ogwen

| 0 | | 1 km | 1 mile |

▲ Map: Explorer OL 17
▲ Distance: 4.5 km/2¾ miles
▲ Walk ID: 757 Peter Salenieks

Difficulty rating

Time

▲ Mountains, Lake/Loch, Toilets, Great Views

Twll Du (Devil's Kitchen) from Ogwen Cottage

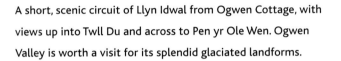

A historic view of the falls at Twll Du (Devil's Kitchen).

A short, scenic circuit of Llyn Idwal from Ogwen Cottage, with views up into Twll Du and across to Pen yr Ole Wen. Ogwen Valley is worth a visit for its splendid glaciated landforms.

❶ The walk starts at the eastern end of the car park. Follow the stone path south, crossing a double stile and then a wooden footbridge. The path bends round to the left, before swinging back to the right after about 200 m. Follow the path to Llyn Idwal, go through a gate and continue along the eastern side of the lake. After passing Idwal Slabs, the path climbs towards the stream.

❷ Cross the stream and continue more steeply along the path until you reach a path junction beside a large boulder.

❸ For a better view into Twll Du, turn left at the large boulder and ascend a little further. When you have finished, continue along the path in front of the large boulder. Turn north and descend towards Llyn Idwal. Stone slabs bridge several small streams as the path goes along the western side of the lake. Bear right along the northern edge of Llyn Idwal, joining the path from Y Garn just before you reach a wooden footbridge.

❹ Cross the footbridge and turn left at the footpath junction, finally rejoining your outward route back to the car park at Ogwen Cottage.

further information

This walk will take about 90 minutes. While it should present few difficulties in good conditions, this is graded as a moderate walk because the stream crossing can be awkward. Under winter conditions, the upper section is deceptively icy and should only be attempted by suitably experienced and equipped parties.

ANGLESEY

Conwy

Bangor

A55

Caernarfon

Betws-y-Coed

A487

A470

Ogwen Cottage

A5(T)

Llyn Idwal

National Nature Reserve

Twll Du (Devil's Kitchen)

access information

Cars can be parked in the pay-and-display car park at Ogwen Cottage. This is approached from the A5(T), either travelling west from Capel Curig or east from Bethesda. If this car park is full, there are lay-bys beside Llyn Ogwen, a few hundred metres east along the A5(T). There is also a bus service to Ogwen.

0   1 km   1 mile

▲ Map: Explorer OL 23
▲ Distance: 8 km/5 miles
▲ Walk ID: 604 Chris Dixon

Difficulty rating

Time

▲ Mountains, River, Pub, Birds,
Good for Wheelchairs

Mawddach Estuary from Penmaenpool

Following the route of a dismantled railway towards the sea, this walk takes in splendid views of the hilly countryside. The estuary at Barmouth Bridge is a haven for waders and other waterbirds. Parts of the walk pass unspoilt ancient woodland.

1 At the car park you will see a hut and the toll-bridge behind it at the start of the walk. From here, head downstream without crossing the river.

2 Just over a small road is a hotel, converted from the old Penmaenpool railway station. The remainder of this walk is along the course of the old railway as it heads towards the sea.

3 Pass through the gate, and after a slight bend the path heads for a kilometre straight across the marsh before reaching the estuary itself. After a further kilometre, you will cross a footbridge.

4 About 2 km later, you may start to get views of the distant Barmouth Bridge.

5 You can choose to take the road leading to Morfa Mawddach Station (formerly Barmouth Junction), or follow the route down the track on the right and past a disused platform. If you go to the station, a gate at the end of the one remaining platform links back up with the route.

6 Barmouth Bridge can be crossed for a small toll, but since the toll booth is at the far side, you can easily go half way for a view out to sea or back up the estuary. From here, retrace your steps to Penmaenpool.

access information

The walk starts from the car park at Penmaenpool on the A493 west of Dolgellau. It is best to arrive by car, although the walk could be done in reverse from Morfa Mawddach railway station.

Barmouth Bridge spans the Mawddach estuary, a haven for waterbirds. It also offers fine views of Cardigan Bay.

▲ Map: Explorer 262
▲ Distance: 10 km/6¼ miles
▲ Walk ID: 635 Chris Dixon

Difficulty rating

Time

▲ Sea, Toilets, Church, National Trust/NTS, Wildlife, Birds, Great Views

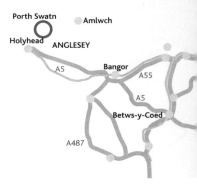

Ynys y Fydlyn from Porth Swtan

This walk begins on the cliffs on Anglesey's north-west coast. After a view of the island of Ynys y Fydlyn the walk heads inland and there is an option to take in one of Anglesey's best viewpoints.

❶ Leave the car park, and head towards the sea. Go through the gate, along the headland. When you reach a junction bear left and keep to the coast. When you reach a stile to the right, cross over it and continue. After a kilometre or so you climb up to a cairn.

❷ From here, dropping down a fairly steep slope, you will reach a bridge. Cross the bridge and take the lesser of two paths, keeping to the left and to the cliffs.

❸ Upon rounding the headland called Trwyn y Cerwyn there is a view of the island, Ynys y Fydlyn. From the beach, looking east, you will see a small marshy lake, and a track climbing to its right. Take the track and keep to the side of the forest. You soon join a track which leads to the road.

❹ When you reach the road, turn left and after about 200 m, you should turn right onto a track to Hen-dy farmhouse. Continue through the gate. Follow the path round the pond in the marshy area ahead, and head for the white gate on the horizon, which will let you into another farm. Go round the back of the building on the left, through another gate, and then up to the far corner of the field, where it meets the road. Turn right along the road.

❺ After about 300 metres, take the path to the left. Head to the left of Myndd y Garn, then turn right across the bottom of the peak. Continue along the path back to the road, and turn left. After a few minutes walking, another road joins from the right. At the next fork turn right and continue on the road to the church.

❻ Follow the road back to Porth Swtan, and turn right to return to the car park.

access information

Access to Porth Swtan is by car via the A5025, off the A5. Park in the car park at Port Swtan.

A lighthouse perches on the barren island of Holyhead, which lies to the north-west of Anglesey, and is connected to it by a rocky causeway.

further information

The island of Ynys y Fydlyn is easily accessible except at high tide. There is a small beach and a large cave.

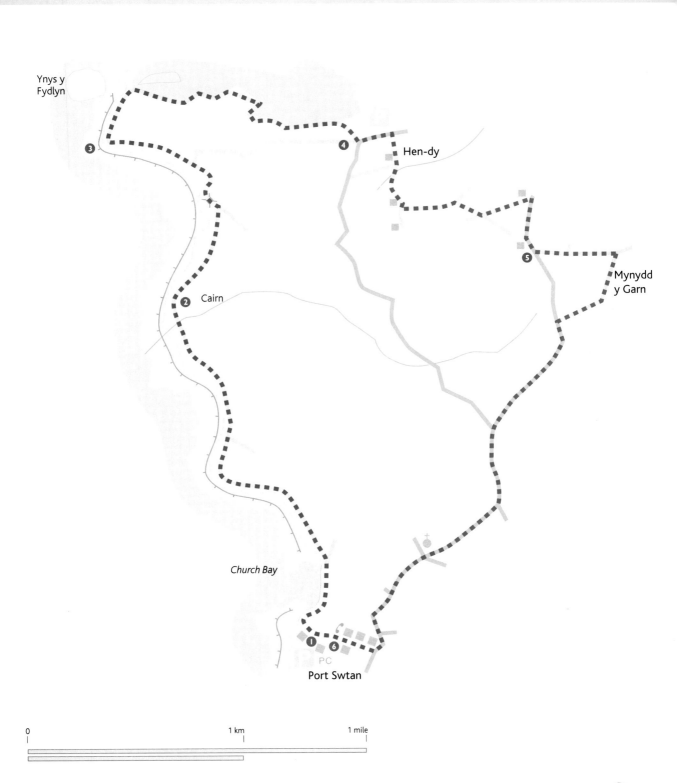

Ynys y
Fydlyn

3

2 Cairn

Church Bay

Hen-dy

4

5

Mynydd
y Garn

1 **6**

P C

Port Swtan

0

1 km

1 mile

▲ Map: Explorer 264
▲ Distance: 22 km/13¾ miles
▲ Walk ID: 753 Jim Grindle

Difficulty rating

‼‼

Time

●●●●●

▲ Sea, Pub, Toilets, Church, Great Views

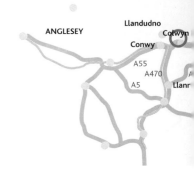

Rhyl from Rhôs-on-Sea (Colwyn Bay)

This is an easy-to-follow linear walk along the coast, using a specially made path as well as promenades and sea walls. It goes from west to east to take advantage of the prevailing wind.

Bodnant Castle boasts one of the finest gardens in Britain, famous for its display of rhododendrons, azaleas and magnolias. Perched above the River Conwy valley, the gardens offer fine views of Snowdonia.

❶ Keep Rhôs-on-Sea Information Centre building on your left to begin the walk. After 2 km you approach Colwyn Bay Pier. After another 2 km you have passed Old Colwyn, and the promenade now turns under the railway. A tarmac path branches off on the left. Follow this path.

❷ In 1 km the path rises by sea defence blocks. After another 3 km you cross a bridge. Keep going now for 5 km.

❸ Once you reach the front at Pensarn the railway station of Pensarn and Abergele is only 500 m further on, should you wish to return to Colwyn Bay. The footpath continues between the wall and the railway.

❹ Head towards Rhyl where there is a group of small buildings. Go through the metal kissing gate and onto a red shale path which winds through the dunes. About 300 m away there is a junction with a tarmac path.

❺ Turn right and go through a gate just in front of the bungalows. Go a little to the right to keep in the same direction down Betws Avenue. Turn to the left into Bryn Avenue. At the end of the road turn right and you will reach the Ferry Inn. The main road is just in front. Turn left and make for the bridge over the River Clwyd. Across the river there is a roundabout. Go straight over, following the sign to the railway station, which is still 2 km away. You can walk alongside the Marine Lake for a little. Keep going until you come to the traffic lights by the police station. The railway station is signposted again from here.

❻ From Rhyl you can return to Colwyn Bay by train or taxi.

access information

By car use the A55 Expressway, turning off at the signs for Llandudno and Rhôs-on-Sea. Turn right at the first two sets of traffic lights and right at the first roundabout. Go straight over the next roundabout and turn right at the next lights. This is Rhôs Road which leads directly to a T-junction by the Information Centre.

Views across Colwyn Bay make this a footpath to remember.

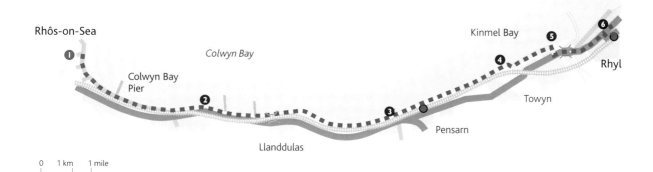

Rhôs-on-Sea

❶

Colwyn Bay

Colwyn Bay
Pier

❷

Llanddulas

❸

Pensarn

Kinmel Bay

❺

❹

Towyn

Rhyl

❻

0   1 km   1 mile

▲ Map: Explorer 164

▲ Distance: 11 km/6³/₄ miles

▲ Walk ID: 981 John Thorn

Difficulty rating

Time

River, Sea, Castle, Birds, Great Views, Café, Food Shop, Good for Kids, Moor, Public Transport, Woodland, Ancient Monument

Three Cliffs Bay from Penmaen

This is a circular walk from Penmaen through the woods and moorland to Three Cliffs Bay on the south coast of the Gower peninsula, a designated area of outstanding natural beauty.

❶ Follow the track up the ridge. When you pass a stone marked 'Gower Way 12', bear right, following the track that skirts the woodland to your right. Just before the path divides, cross the stile on your right and follow the path into the woods as it opens out into a wider track. After a right-hand bend, go straight ahead at a crossroads (passing Gower Way stone 14).

❷ At the crossroads at the bottom of a valley, turn right, following the track down. (Opposite on the left is Gower Way stone 15). The remnants of a prehistoric burial chamber will soon appear on your right.

❸ Go through the gateway following a yellow arrow. Ignore the road on the left but turn left at the T-junction. On reaching the Gower Heritage Centre, continue straight ahead and cross the footbridge on the left. Continue along the road until you reach the main road.

❹ Pass Shepherd's shop on your left and a house on your right. Turn right onto a path by a field gate. After 20 m, cross the footbridge and turn right, following a blue arrow. The path bears left over a hill. Ignore the left-hand path and continue ahead. The path opens out with a view of Pennard Castle. Continue down the left-hand side of the valley.

❺ As you near the beach, continue ahead until you reach a ridge of pebbles, then turn right along the ridge and cross the stepping-stones. Do not take the path ahead marked by an arrow but turn left. Continue around the edge of the marsh with the hedge on your right. Go to the left of the sand dunes and emerge onto the beach.

❻ Take the path to the top of the dunes. Follow the path that climbs up on the right-hand side of the holiday cottages. When you reach a stony track turn left, then turn right onto the road. Turn left at the T-junction. Cross the main road in front of the church and return to the start of the walk by following the narrow road on the right.

access information

Follow the A4118 along the Gower. Shortly after the Gower Inn at the Penmaen sign on the left-hand side, with the church in front of you, turn right on the narrow road. Follow this for about 200 yards, passing the care home on your left. When the road bears left, bear right onto the rough track and park on the grass.

Penmaen is accessible by bus, service 18 from Swansea.

The view from the cliffs at Three Cliffs Bay in Swansea makes the climb up the sand dunes worthwhile.

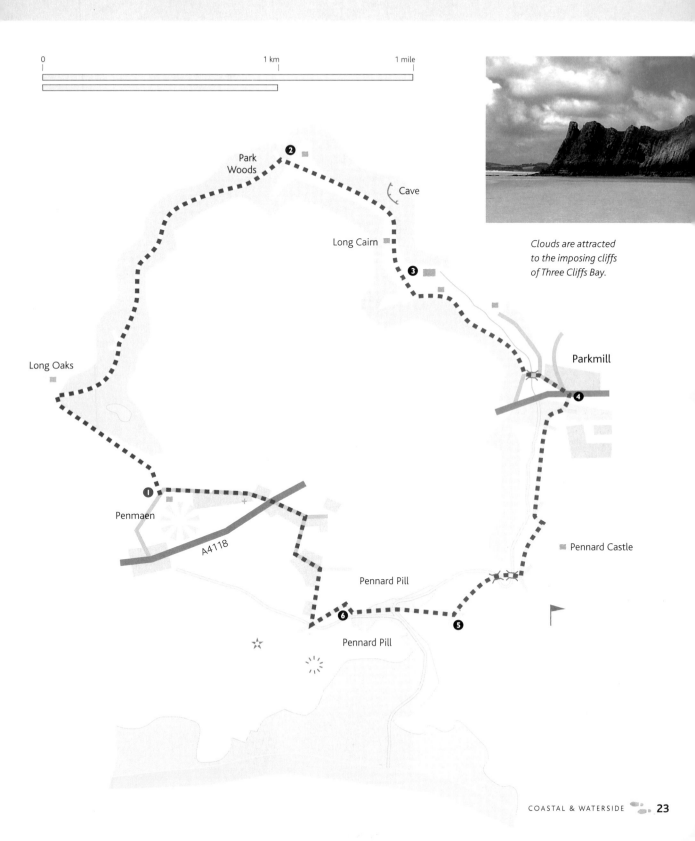

0　　　　　　　　　　　　　　　1 km　　　　　　　　　　1 mile

Park Woods

Cave

Long Cairn

Parkmill

Long Oaks

Penmaen

A4118

Pennard Castle

Pennard Pill

Pennard Pill

❶ ❷ ❸ ❹ ❺ ❻

Clouds are attracted to the imposing cliffs of Three Cliffs Bay.

Difficulty rating

Time

▲ Hills or Fells, Sea, Pub, Toilets, National Trust, Birds, Flowers, Great Views, Café, Gift Shop, Public Transport, Ancient Monument

Burry Holms from Rhossili

This walk demonstrates much of the natural beauty of the Gower. From Rhossili, climb the Beacon, descend to Llangennith, cross the dunes to the beach, explore Burry Holms and return along the beach.

1 From the car park entrance, walk to the left of a house with a white garage door, then turn left and follow the path around the church. Turn left, following the lane slightly downhill. Go through the gate marked 'Rhossili Down' and bear slightly right up the hill. After about 250 m the track levels out a bit. Bear slightly right then left to reach the trig point.

2 Continue along the grassy track in the general direction of Llangennith, bearing left along the ridge. Where the path divides, bear left, aiming for the hilltop ahead with a rocky crag. From the top, follow the grassy track ahead with the steep hill down on your left. Ignore the path on the left.

3 At a junction with a smaller path, turn right, heading in the direction of the large grey barn on the far hill. After 100 m, cross another path and bear left across the valley. Follow the path, making for the right-hand side of the small clump of trees to join a rough lane. Go through a gate, cross a stream and follow the road ahead into Llangennith.

4 Turn left on the road following the sign marked 'Beach'. At the junction go ahead, following the road towards Broughton.

5 At the entrance to the caravan park, cross the cattle grid and take the track on the left. After 150 m cross a stile. Just over the brow of the hill bear right. Cross another stile then fork right on the less well-defined path. Cross a fence at a stile and continue across the dunes. Turn right on the beach.

6 Burry Holms Island can be reached at low tide. Having explored the island, retrace your steps to the beach and continue along the beach towards Rhossili. Just before the end of the beach, climb the steps to the left. After 100 m, turn right through a gate and continue uphill. Pass between the buildings to return to the car park.

At high tide Burry Holms is inaccessible, although exploration of the island is possible when the sea retreats at low tide.

further information

• Do not follow this walk in poor visibility. Apart from missing the best views, some navigation depends on sighting far-away points.

• As you climb towards the trig point (point 2), you may see Lundy Island. Left of this is Clovelly, Ilfracombe and Exmoor as far as Minehead. To the right of Lundy are Pembroke and Tenby.

• Burry Holms has an Iron Age fort and various other relics.

This walk takes in a variety of interesting archaeological features including an Iron Age fort, as well as beautiful countryside.

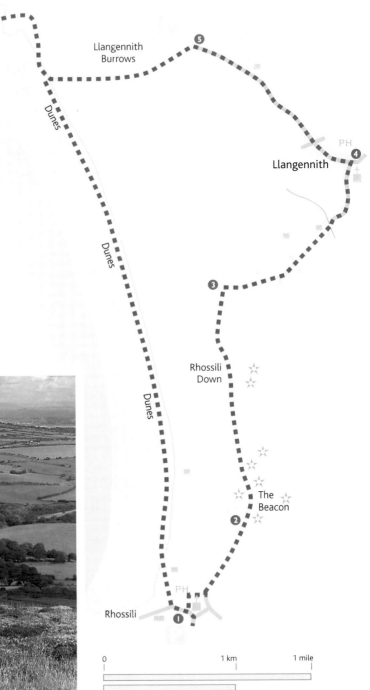

▲ Map: Explorer 164
▲ Distance: 8 km/5 miles
▲ Walk ID: 148 N. Rudd-Jones

Difficulty rating

Time

▲ Sea, Toilets, National
Trust, Wildlife, Flowers, Great Views

Mewslade Bay from Rhossili

This is a glorious walk combining cliffs with wild beaches and a bird's-eye view of the Gower peninsula from Rhossili Down. If conditions are right, you can visit the enticingly named Worms Head.

❶ Turn left onto the path by the visitor centre. Go through the gate and head left towards Worms Head. When the path curves left, cross the grass to the building ahead. Take the grassy path to the southern cliffs. You will soon reach a corner of dry-stone wall on the left – keep alongside it.

❷ Turn right just before the gate at the corner of the wall; turn left and follow the wall again. At the next corner turn left. At the junction continue uphill. At the top follow the path along the wall. Continue along the cliff, keeping the wall on your left. Ignore the path to the right above Fall Bay. On reaching a ladder over the wall, do not climb it – follow the middle path. Take the steep path next to the wire fence. Follow the wall towards Mewslade Bay.

❸ At the sharp cliffs, head away from the wall. At what looks like a deserted stone shepherd's hut, head uphill. As the white house comes into view to the right, take the grassy path inland.

❹ Take the right-hand path opposite the rocky outcrop. Do not cross the stile, but turn right. Continue uphill on the left-hand side of the path. Go through the gate into the woods. Pass through a farm and turn left onto a road. Turn right at the larger road and immediately left at the post box. At the fork take the left track past a house called Bramwood.

❺ 100 m before the large white house, climb the stile into the Nature Reserve. Follow the path across a footbridge, pass a house on the left, then another stile, to go uphill. Climb the stile and cross a minor road to take the track opposite. Skirt around the reservoir and follow the track left to Rhossili Down. At the fork stay on the wider track to the right to reach a trig point with spectacular views.

❻ Retrace your steps for 50 m then take the right fork to Rhossili village. At the corner of the wall, head straight on. At the next corner take the path downhill to the gate. Follow the track. Just before St Mary's Church, take the path to the right. Follow the road to the car park.

access information

The walk starts from the car park at Rhossili, at the end of the B4247 west of the A4118.

Buses 18, 18A, 18C, 18D run to Rhossili from Swansea; call First Cymru for information on 0870 6082608.

Halfway around this circular footpath, you will be rewarded with beautiful views over Mewslade Bay.

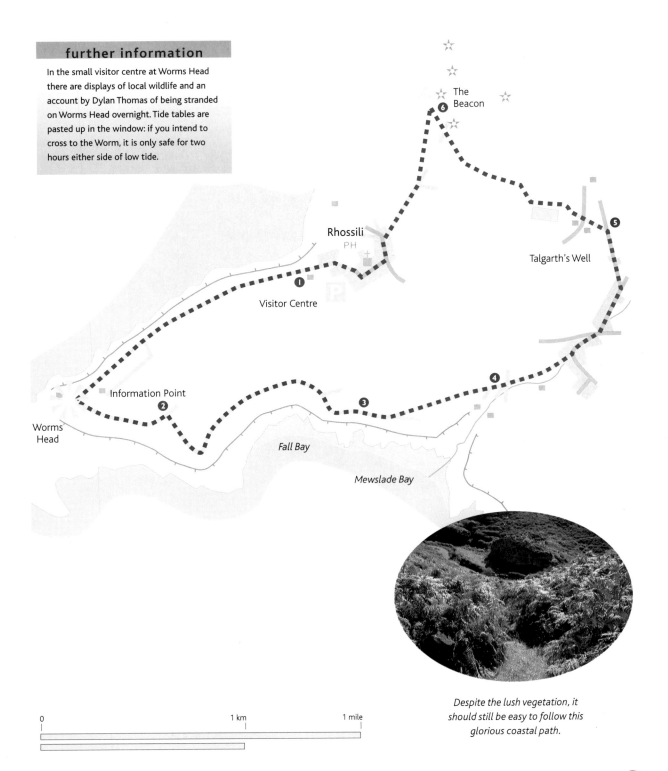

further information

In the small visitor centre at Worms Head there are displays of local wildlife and an account by Dylan Thomas of being stranded on Worms Head overnight. Tide tables are pasted up in the window: if you intend to cross to the Worm, it is only safe for two hours either side of low tide.

The
Beacon

6

Rhossili

PH

5

Talgarth's Well

Visitor Centre

1

Information Point

2

3

4

Worms
Head

Fall Bay

Mewslade Bay

Despite the lush vegetation, it
should still be easy to follow this
glorious coastal path.

0   1 km   1 mile

▲ Map: Explorer OL 36
▲ Distance: 1.5 km/1 mile
▲ Walk ID: 1089 Peter Salenieks

Difficulty rating

Time

▲ Sea, Toilets, National Trust, Wildlife, Birds, Flowers, Great Views, Gift Shop, Mostly Flat, Public Transport, Ancient Monument

Martin's Haven & Marine Nature Reserve

This is a scenic circuit of the headland at Martin's Haven, offering views of Skomer Island and Skokholm Island and opportunities for watching seals within the Marine Nature Reserve.

❶ Exit the National Trust car park at the far corner. Walk down a few steps, then turn left and follow the road downhill towards Martin's Haven. Just before the road bends right, go through the kissing gate and turn left. Follow a grassy path, which runs parallel to the stone wall, until you see a stile near the cliff edge, overlooking Deadman's Bay.

❷ The path leads clockwise around the tip of the Marloes Peninsula. After the path bears around to the right, a natural arch can be seen, connecting two coves on the edge of the peninsula. About 200 m after the arch, the path joins a footpath, which leads to Wooltack Point, the northern tip of the peninsula.

❸ Retrace your route from Wooltack Point and bear left, following the footpath along the northern edge of the peninsula, before bearing right and climbing a small hill to reach the old coastguard lookout.

❹ Continue along the footpath until you reach steps leading down to the kissing gate. Go through the kissing gate and follow the road back uphill, passing Lockley Lodge Information Point, to reach the National Trust car park.

access information

The National Trust car park at Martin's Haven is accessible by road from Haverfordwest via the B4327 and a minor road through Marloes. Martin's Haven can also be reached by the Puffin Shuttle Bus Service 400, which operates between St David's and Milford Haven.

This footpath offers both rugged cliff views and a chance to spot grey seals.

Wooltack Point

Haven Point

Martin's Haven

Jack Sound

The Anvil

Deadman's Bay

0   1 km   1 mile

▲ Map: Explorer OL 35
▲ Distance: 7 km/4¼ miles
▲ Walk ID: 1411 Pat Roberts

Difficulty rating

Time

▲ Sea, Toilets, Wildlife, Birds, Flowers, Great Views, Butterflies, Woodland

Witches Cauldron from Moylgrove

This walk is a lovely mixture of coast and countryside, taking in two woodland areas.

❶ From the car park walk right along the road towards St Dogmaels. Follow the road as it climbs. Where the road swings sharply right, look for a gate on the left. Pass through the gate and walk down through Cwm Trewyddel, following the stream. The path goes over a small bridge and up to join the minor road from Moylgrove.

❷ Follow the road round the bend and up the hill for about 120 m. Follow the 'Coast Path' sign on the right, and continue with the sea on your right.

❸ Pwll y Wrach (The Witches Cauldron) is a classic example of marine erosion. The path drops right down and climbs sharply back up, passing over a natural arch on the way. The sea comes in under the arch, creating the 'boiling cauldron'. Follow the path down the steps and back up the other side.

❹ After the climb you come to a double stile. Leave the coast by the left-hand stile. The route continues over fields initially. After passing a ruined building, enter the woodland of Cwm Ffynnon-alwm to emerge over a stile and turn left onto a green track. This soon becomes a stony farm track climbing gradually.

❺ Continue through a gate opposite Treriffith Farm where the sign points right, past the farm buildings then left up the drive. Emerge through a gate and continue to reach the Moylgrove road.

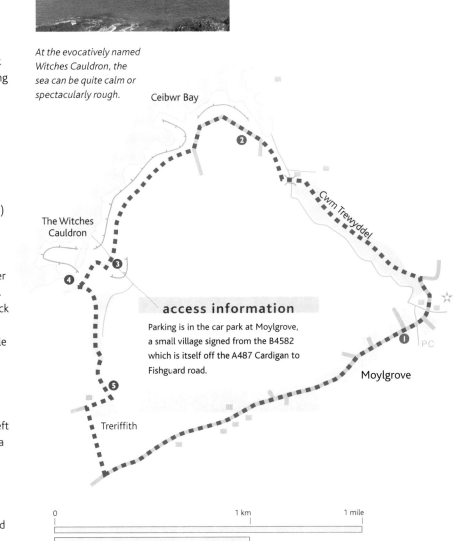

At the evocatively named Witches Cauldron, the sea can be quite calm or spectacularly rough.

access information

Parking is in the car park at Moylgrove, a small village signed from the B4582 which is itself off the A487 Cardigan to Fishguard road.

▲ Map: Explorer OL 35
▲ Distance: 9 km/5¹/₂ miles
▲ Walk ID: 976 D. J. Martin

Difficulty rating

Time

▲ Sea, Toilets, National Trust, Birds, Flowers, Great Views, Café, Food Shop, Ancient Monument

Around St David's Head

This circular walk around St David's Head includes part of the Pembrokeshire Coast Path. There is a short optional diversion from the Coast Path onto Penllechwen Head, which gives extensive coastal views.

1 Leaving the car park, walk up the road, past the first turn on the left. At a marker on the right, turn left up a road. At the top, follow the main track right, towards Upper Porthmawr. After about 100 m the track turns left. Continue past the farmhouse.

2 Above the farmhouse the main track turns left. At this point, just before a small quarry, follow the path off to the right, taking in excellent views of Whitesands Bay, Ramsey Island and St Bride's Bay. At the T-junction, turn right through the gate.

3 A short distance downhill the main track continues straight on, but the walk turns left, behind a low building at a three-way marker, and immediately crosses a stile with another marker. Continue along the bottom of the field, keeping the stone wall on your right, and cross a stile. The next stile, near a farmhouse, crosses onto a track. Turn left to go to the top of the ridge. At the gate follow the track round to the right. Follow the public footpath indicated by the marker. Where the path becomes indistinct, head left of the hill and aim for a gate and stile in the top right of the field. Cross the stile and continue towards a marker.

4 Turn right and follow the track downhill, passing through a metal gate. When you reach a wooden gate, turn to the left onto a grassy track at the bottom of the field. Keep the fence on your right, ignoring side tracks.

5 At the T-junction, turn left up the hill, with a stone wall on your right. The path continues uphill and then between rocky outcrops. Descend towards the sea.

6 When you reach the Pembrokeshire Coast Path, turn left. Keep to the track that is closest to the coast. At Porthmelgan climb up the wooden steps on the path and continue back to Whitesands Bay.

access information

Take the B4583 from St David's towards Whitesands Bay. Whitesands Bay car park is at the end of this road.

A picturesque spot on the Pembrokeshire Coast Path is home to the St Justinian's lifeboat station, which serves the St David's Head area.

Markers point the way along the Coast Path to make navigation extremely easy.

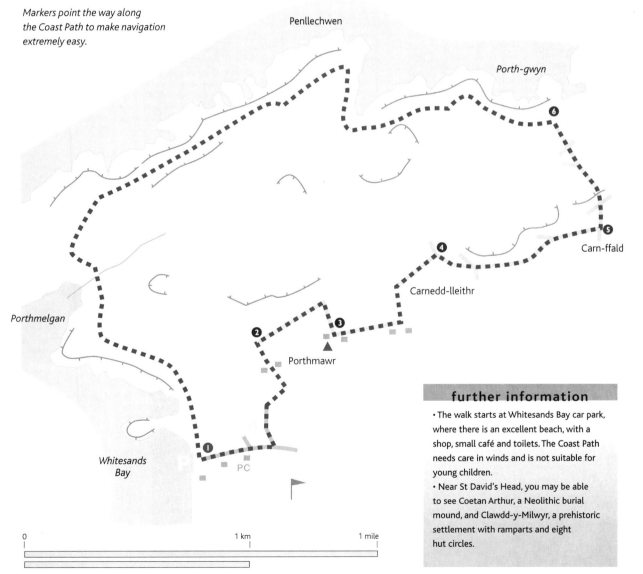

Penllechwen

Porth-gwyn

6

5 Carn-ffald

4

Carnedd-lleithr

Porthmelgan

2

3

Porthmawr

1

Whitesands Bay

PC

further information

• The walk starts at Whitesands Bay car park, where there is an excellent beach, with a shop, small café and toilets. The Coast Path needs care in winds and is not suitable for young children.

• Near St David's Head, you may be able to see Coetan Arthur, a Neolithic burial mound, and Clawdd-y-Milwyr, a prehistoric settlement with ramparts and eight hut circles.

0   1 km   1 mile

▲ Map: Explorer OL 35
▲ Distance: 7 km/4¼ miles
▲ Walk ID: 1414 Pat Roberts

Difficulty rating

Time

▲ Sea, Pub, Toilets, Wildlife, Birds, Flowers, Great Views, Butterflies, Waterfall, Woodland

Cwm Rhigian Woods from Parrog

Walk part of the Pembrokeshire Coast Path, and enjoy the wildlife in Cwm Rhigian Woods, before walking open moorland and returning to Newport and Parrog.

❶ From the car park, join the coast path by going down the slipway and left, with the sea on your right. If the tide is in, keep above the sea wall and follow the 'High Tide Route' as signed. Follow the Coast Path for over 2 km. Pass the old lifeboat station and Cat Rock. There is lovely scenery to enjoy here, and plenty of sea birds to look out for.

❷ As you drop down into the cove at Aber Rhigian, cross the stream using the footbridge and follow the footpath away from the sea. Soon recross the stream so that it is now on your right-hand side. The stream cascades down and just after a good waterfall, the path swings left, and over another footbridge. Emerge from the wood over a stile, and at a bungalow turn left up the drive. When you reach a T-Junction with another track, turn right up to the A487. Head left for 200 m.

❸ Turn right up the drive to the Hendre. After the farmhouse, go through a gate and carry onto cross a stream. Follow the sign along the left hedge of this field to another stile. Continue straight on up the track, keeping to the right of the hedge to reach a broken stile. Go straight on.

❹ Climb over the stile and continue on up ahead to a wall, which you keep on your right-hand side to soon walk between two walls. Cross a minor road

and continue past a house and through a small gate onto open moorland. Take the left path at the signpost. When you reach the next fork, keep left to continue down a road and over, turning left over a cattle grid towards Newport.

❺ Emerge at the bottom of Mill Lane and take the short cut up the side of the church to reach the A487 at Newport. Head left for 120 m and take the signed road down to the right to the start of the walk at Parrog.

It is possible to see across Newport Sands to St Brynach's Church, home to a 4-metre, elaborately patterned Celtic cross, believed to be the finest in Wales.

further information

While walking down the long descent into Newport, notice the mill stream down on the right side of the road, and the remains of Castle Mill next to the bridge near the bottom.

Park in Parrog car park, at the yacht club. Parrog is signed from the A487 in Newport.

A good bus service serves Newport from Fishguard or Cardigan.

The area is renowned for its scenery and birdlife, and at low tide it is a joy to geologists.

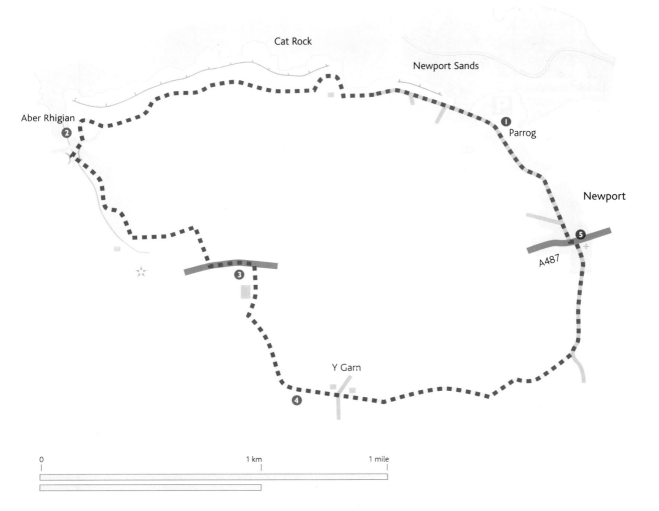

Cat Rock

Newport Sands

Aber Rhigian

2

1

Parrog

Newport

5

A487

3

Y Garn

4

0   1 km   1 mile

- ▲ Map: Explorer OL 12
- ▲ Distance: 9.5 km/6 miles
- ▲ Walk ID: 1499 John Thorn

Difficulty rating

Time

▲ Hills or Fells, River, Pub, Wildlife, Birds, Great Views, Butterflies, Industrial Archaeology, Moor, Public Transport, Waterfall, Woodland

Hepste Waterfalls from Pontneddfechan

This walk gives a taste of the 'Waterfall Country' south of Ystadfellte – including Sgwd yr Eira where you can walk under the falls – with some moorland sections and great views.

1 From the car park, walk back over the bridge. After 30 m turn sharp right in front of the houses onto a gravel track. Continue along the track, ignoring turns left and right. Opposite the ruins of the Gunpowder Works cross the footbridge. Go straight ahead up a narrow path, and continue up some steps. Turn left at the signs towards Sgwd yr Eira, going through a gate and following the path between spruce trees.

2 Turn right following the 'Advised Path' signs, then left after about 50 m.

3 Turn left at the signpost to Sgwd yr Eira. The path drops steeply down some steps and then there is a short, rocky section before the falls. You can walk under the falls here. Retrace your steps back to the signpost, then follow the signs to Penderyn.

4 Bear right up the hill, keeping the fence on your left. Look out for views to the tops of the Brecon Beacons on your left. Just over the crest of the hill, cross a stile on your left but continue in the same general direction downhill for 50 m to cross another stile. Follow the well-defined track, passing some quarries on your right. Pass a stile on your left and follow the wide track (an old railway). Go through a kissing gate and follow the lane to the road. Turn right onto the road and go steeply uphill, passing a children's playground.

5 Continue ahead, ignoring a junction on your left, and follow the road downhill. Where the road turns left, go straight ahead through a gate. Follow this track for about 1.5 km.

6 The path descends past some old workings on the right and crosses a shallow valley. Ignore the path on your left and follow the path ahead. Continue down to the starting point.

On this walk the tranquillity of the countryside contrasts with the thunderous roar of the waterfalls.

access information

This walk starts at the 'waterfalls' car park in Pontneddfechan. Turn off the A465 at the A4109 junction then turn right at the lights. The X5 bus service from Swansea goes to the car park.

It is possible to walk behind the wall of rushing water formed by the Sgwd yr Eira waterfalls.

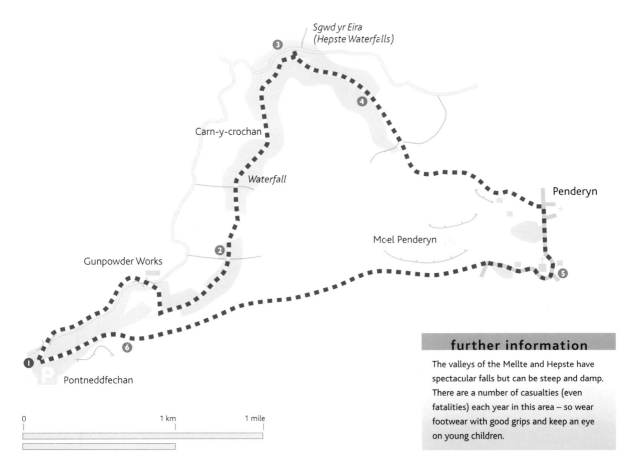

further information

The valleys of the Mellte and Hepste have spectacular falls but can be steep and damp. There are a number of casualties (even fatalities) each year in this area – so wear footwear with good grips and keep an eye on young children.

▲ Map: Explorer 265
▲ Distance: 9 km/5½ miles
▲ Walk ID: 342 Jim Grindle

Difficulty rating

Time

River, Pub, Toilets, Play Area, Wildlife, Flowers, Great Views, Good for Wheelchairs

Loggerheads and the Leete Path

Loggerheads is not far from Mold and is a Country Park. The walk takes you through the park and along a terrace above the River Alyn. Field paths and country lanes bring you back to the Leete Path near the start.

❶ Cross the little bridge at the end of the car park. Pass by some buildings and continue to a stone bridge over the River Alyn. Go over the bridge and turn left towards a gate at the end of the country park signposted Leete Path. The gravelled track becomes muddier and the channel of the Leete is to your right. Pass the boarding kennels and continue on their driveway past a white metal gate to a lane. Cross to another signpost.

❷ You come to a diagonal crossing of tracks. Take the north-west path that keeps you on the same level. You will notice a number of mine shafts on the right and will shortly cross a bridge over the largest shaft. Another diagonal crossroads is reached and then a signposted junction with another right of way.

❸ Following this you come to a lane. Turn left, downhill, and cross the road bridge. On a sharp right bend, follow the footpath sign to Pentre on the left.

❹ Cross six stiles, keeping to the left-hand edge of the fields. The seventh takes you to the other side of the wire and the next down to a junction with a bridleway. Turn right and go up the hill with the cascade from a small lake on your left. You come to a lane where you turn left. Pass Wayside Cottage and turn left at the T-junction.

❺ Walk for about 2 km, then look right to see the Jubilee Tower on Moel Fammau. Continue until a concrete road to the left takes you down to a ford and bridge. Cross the river and climb towards a signpost 'Leete Path, Loggerheads' on the right, just where the lane bends left.

❻ Take the right turn, and retrace your steps to the car park, 1.5 km away.

This footpath leads you through such tranquil countryside that it is difficult to believe that the area was once an industrial landscape of mine-shafts, waterwheels and the water channel called the Leete.

Loggerheads Country Park lies 5 km to the west of Mold on the A494. Parking is by the Information Centre. The Ruthin/Mold bus service calls in at the car park.

The Leete was a clay-lined channel, designed to carry water that had been pumped from the lead mines in the adjacent valley to prevent flooding. It runs alongside the River Alyn for a distance of about 5 kilometres.

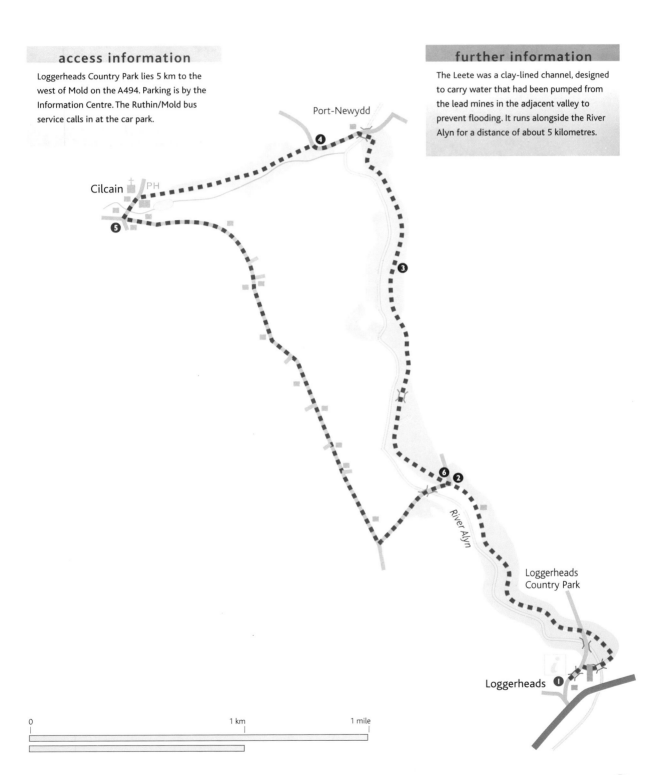

Port-Newydd

Cilcain

River Alyn

Loggerheads Country Park

Loggerheads

0   1 km   1 mile

▲ Map: Explorer 256
▲ Distance: 9 km/5½ miles
▲ Walk ID: 230 Jim Grindle

Difficulty rating

Time

●●

▲ River, Toilets, National Trust/NTS, Good for Wheelchairs (accessible for part of the way)

Erddig Hall at Wrexham Steeple

This is a short, pleasant walk through the grounds surrounding Erddig Hall, a National Trust property. It includes riverside, parkland and woodland sections and is mostly easy underfoot.

❶ Come out of the car park and turn right. Walk towards the crossroads. Go straight across, as far as a signpost by the railings on the left. Join a newly tarred track downhill. After passing a cattle grid you will see the Cup and Saucer Waterfall to your left. Continue on the track, crossing over a bridge. The path will then lead you on to a second, larger bridge.

Erddig Hall provides a majestic backdrop to this footpath, which runs through the grounds that surround the house.

access information

Erddig Hall is 3 km south of Wrexham and is well signposted from the A483 and the A525.

further information

The tower of the Parish Church of St Giles in Wrexham is among the Seven Wonders of Wales. It is a short drive from Erddig Hall.

2 Cross the bridge and go through the kissing gate on the right. Follow the track by the river to reach a car park on a lane. Turn right on to the lane, and just before the road signs, turn left through a gate.

3 Follow the river bank or the hedge on the left of the fields. Watch out for a footbridge to cross. Follow the white arrows on the signposts, which lead you gradually above the river, but stay in the wood with the river below you on the right. Cross a bridge and stile near the edge of the wood and follow the track to the edge of a meadow.

4 Make for the large tree. If you look upwards you will see another signpost just past a second tree, a large oak. At the top of the slope keep to the right edge of the field – the exit is through a stile to the right.

5 Cross the stile to the lane, turn left and cross to a kissing gate. Continue on the narrow path ahead with fields on your left. You will reach a signpost. Keep straight ahead until you come to the end of the fields on the left. Turn left where the paths meet. Go left again, still with the fields on your left and the grounds of Erddig on your right.

6 Keep on the path until you come to a gate. Turn right and go through another gate. You will see ahead of you the dovecote by the car park as you return to the start of the walk.

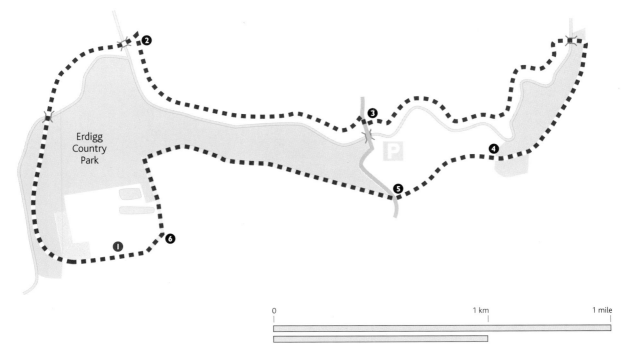

Erdigg Country Park

| 0 | | 1 km | 1 mile |

▲ Map: Explorer OL 17
▲ Distance: 14 km/8¾ miles
▲ Walk ID: 338 Haydn Williams

Difficulty rating

Time

▲ Pub, Castle, Great Views

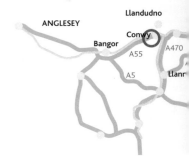

Tal-y-Fan

This walk takes you over the northern part of the Carneddau range. Allow yourself time at the summit to enjoy this glorious landscape and also views of Anglesey, Liverpool and the Conwy Valley.

❶ From the car park follow the black track for half a kilometre. The way the tracks diverge is slightly confusing, but you should turn sharp right and follow the obvious track uphill. Keep the lake to your right and continue for half a kilometre, to meet a farmer's track.

❷ Turn right on to this track and stay on it until you reach a wall on the left, following it for about 2.5 km. Cross the ford, then continue uphill, keeping the wall on the right for 200 m. Pick up the track immediately ahead. Continue for about one kilometre, from where you will see a wall 90 degrees to your right.

❸ Turning right at this wall, and by keeping it on your left, you will start a steep climb for 200 m. On reaching the summit cross the ladder stile to the trig point.

❹ At the summit enjoy the extensive views of the Menai Straits, Anglesey, Puffin Island, Conwy Bay, Great Orme, Llandudno Bay, Conwy Castle and Conwy Valley. Recross the ladder stile and go directly downhill with the wall at your back. When you reach a small cairn, turn right on to a footpath that takes you back to the wall. Follow this until you reach a distinct corner of the wall.

❺ From this point pick your own path down to the quarry heading diagonally right for half a kilometre. At the quarry take the left-hand route down. After approximately 200 m a stream drops off to the right. Continue straight on and turn right at the next obvious path.

❻ Walk past the standing stone and this path will bring you back to your original track. Turn left and follow the track back to the car park.

The windswept ridges of the Welsh mountains offer panoramic views to take the breath away.

Conwy is on the A55 near Llandudno. By car from Conwy town square, turn left before the arch, proceed uphill to another arch and follow the road to the right, going uphill for 2 km. Go over the cattle grid and, ignoring the small car park by the road junction, carry on uphill. After a bend on the road you will see a well-built wall with a parking sign. Turn left here into the car park. To come by public transport use the Sherpa Park & Ride.

Pengychnant

Craigytedwen

From the highest point of this walk you will have excellent views of Conwy, with its magnificent castle and a bridge (below) built to complement the style of the fortress.

Standing Stone

Tal-y-Fan

0   1 km   1 mile

▲ Map: Explorer OL 23
▲ Distance: 6 km/3¾ miles
▲ Walk ID: 225 Ian Morison

Difficulty rating

Time

▲ Hills or Fells, Lake/Loch, Toilets,
Wildlife, Birds, Great Views

The Precipice Walk, north of Dolgellau

A classic Snowdonia walk with wonderful vistas over the Arans, Coed y Brenin Forest, the Mawddach estuary and Cader Idris. The view is one of the most beautiful panoramas in Wales, and there are perfect spots for picnics.

1 Turn left out of the car park and follow the minor road for a short way. Turn left along the signposted track. Follow it round to the right where the track splits into two, keeping the open field to your left. Bear left as you pass the stone cottage.

2 Cross a low ladder stile into woodland and turn right along the path. Cross the stile at the end of the wood into the open country. Follow the path round to the right. Llyn Cynwch is seen down the valley on the left.

3 Turn right at the corner of the field following the signpost direction. Cross the ladder stile. The village of Llanfachreth is seen in the valley to your right. As you follow the stony path round to the left, Coed y Brenin Forest stretches out in front of you.

4 The narrow path takes you along the flanks of Foel Cynwch. To the right lies the River Mawddach. The view opens out with the Mawddach estuary becoming visible to the right with distant views of Cader Idris.

5 Climb over a ladder stile and follow the path round the hillside to the left. Cross a further ladder stile. Follow the path down towards Llyn Cynwch.

6 Bear left, and drop on to the path by the lake. Follow the path beside the lake. Rejoin the outward route and retrace your steps to the car park.

further information

The route runs high above the River Mawddach. The ground drops steeply into the valley so young children will need to be well supervised, but there are no sheer drops. The path is good, but occasionally rocky.

access information

By car only. A National Park car park is on the left-hand side of the minor road between Dolgellau, on the A470, and the village of Llanfachreth – from Dolgellau, follow signs to the Precipice Walk.

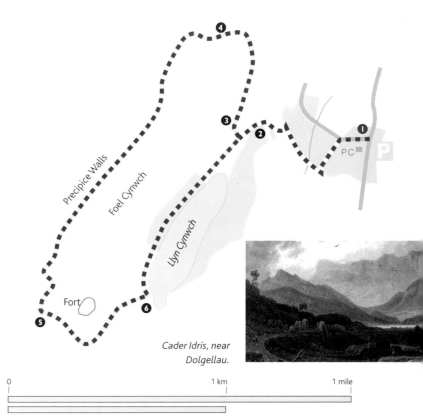

Cader Idris, near Dolgellau.

0   1 km   1 mile

▲ Map: Explorer OL 17
▲ Distance: 8 km/5 miles
▲ Walk ID: 738 Jim Grindle

Difficulty rating

Time

▲ National Trust/NTS,
Great Views, Toilets

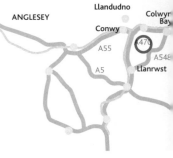

Bodnant Gardens & Moel Gyffylog

This walk begins at the attractive National Trust gardens at Bodnant. It covers the unclassified lanes to the east, rising to 250 m and offering outstanding views over the Conwy valley to the Carneddau range.

❶ Turn left out of the car park at Bodnant. In 300 m you will come to a lane, Ffordd Bodnant. Turn left here and left again at the T-junction just ahead. The lane goes uphill for 1.4 km to a junction just past Bodnant Ucha farm.

❷ Turn right. In 350 m you reach a junction with another lane. Turn left here. Pass a junction with a lane from the left and continue to a small farm, Erw Goch. Barely 100 m further on there is another T-junction.

❸ Turn right with the telephone lines on your right. At the top of the rise is another farm and 100 m beyond it you reach another T-junction. Turn left and go only 50 m, to a lane coming in from the right.

❹ Turn right here for the next junction, 800 m away. Turn right at the signpost in the direction of Eglwysbach. It is 2.5 km downhill to the village, and you cross the stream by the entrance to Gyffylog farm on the way.

❺ Turn right in Eglwysbach, to pass a bus stop on the left and a chapel on the right. Eight hundred metres from the junction you reach a red telephone box and a bus shelter by a crossroads in the hamlet of Graig. Bodnant is signposted on the right. Keep straight on, passing the bus shelter on your left.

❻ Follow the road to Bodnant, to visit the gardens or return to the car park.

further information

The café, car park and the garden centre are free to enter but there is an entrance fee to the gardens themselves (NT members go in free). In addition to the beautiful gardens, there are many semi-wild areas and ponds. The grounds are open every day from mid-March to early November.

access information

Bodnant is on the A470 south of Llandudno and is well signposted from the A55. A bus from Conwy stops outside the gardens.

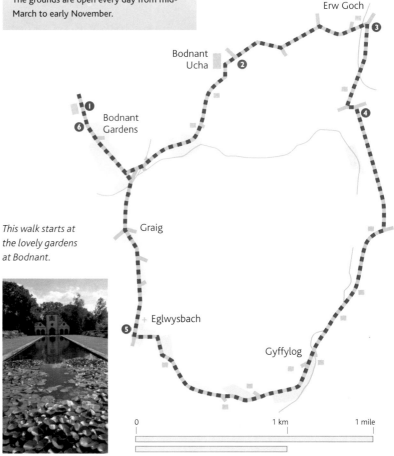

This walk starts at the lovely gardens at Bodnant.

▲ Map: Explorer OL 17
▲ Distance: 6 km/3¾ miles
▲ Walk ID: 772 Hadyn Williams

Difficulty rating

Time

▲ Mountains, Lake/Loch, Great Views

Beddgelert Forest

ANGLESEY

Bangor

Caernarfon

A5

Betws-y-Coe

A4085

A470

A487

Porthmadog

This walk through Beddgelert Forest gives great views of the surrounding mountains. It is easy to follow the route with the aid of the numbered marker poles set at regular intervals through the forest.

❶ At the top of the car park, take a shortcut to the track, through the bushes. Turn left on to the track. Turn right at the first junction, at marker pole 80. Follow the delightful little stream on your right. On your right you have views of Moel Hebog. Turn right on to the concrete bridge. Straight ahead are views of Y Garn.

❷ Look for marker pole 64 and turn left. There is a view of Yr Aran. Carry on uphill keeping the stream on your right. Ahead is the Nantlle Ridge, on the left is Moel Hebog and Moel Ogof.

❸ Turn left at the T-junction and cross a concrete bridge. Turn sharp right on to a footpath, ignoring the junction ahead. Look for a marker pole 66. Bear left on to the track at marker pole 34. Take the path to the right. Bear left at the junction, cross over a concrete bridge at marker pole 42, and carry straight on, ignoring the turning to the right.

❹ Keep bearing left, ignoring the track on your right and the grassy path ahead. Turn left and go downhill at the junction at marker pole 36.

❺ Carry on downhill. Turn right on to the main track, passing marker pole 35. Pass marker pole 34 on your left.

❻ Turn left at the junction, heading downhill. Directly ahead is Moel Hebog, marked by marker pole 33. Turn right at the junction marked by marker pole 70.

This 1831 engraving of Beddgelert captures the beauty and tranquillity of the area.

Afon Colwyn

Beddgelert Forest

Llyn Llywewn

A4085

0   1 km   1 mile

access information

Access is on the Beddgelert to Caernarfon road (A4085). Turn left into the Forestry Commission access and drive down to the car park.

The village of Beddgelert, at the confluence of the Glaslyn and Colwyn rivers, is also situated at the approaches to two mountain passes, offering access to some of the most spectacular scenery in Snowdonia.

❼ Carry on downhill and go across another concrete bridge. Turn left on to the path, which borders the lake. You enter the picnic area. On leaving turn right at marker pole 69 on the edge of the lake.

❽ Carry straight on at the crossroads, at marker pole 68. Turn left at junction post marker pole 67. Turn right off the main track by the trees, marker pole 65, and down the cinder path. Turn right just before the concrete bridge sending you down on the path you came up on. Turn left at marker pole 80 and proceed back to the car park.

▲ Map: Explorer 255
▲ Distance: 6 km/3¾ miles
▲ Walk ID: 1015 Jim Grindle

Difficulty rating

!!!

Time

●●●◖

▲ Hills or Fells, Mountains, River, Toilets, Great Views, Food Shop, Moor, Tea Shop, Waterfall

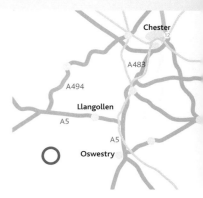

Pistyll Llanrhaeadr and the Berwyns

Starting at a waterfall, this short, circular walk takes you into the fringes of the Berwyn Mountains, where there are clear views of the craggy eastern faces of the highest peaks.

❶ Go through the small wooden gate by the café and turn right towards the falls. Turn right into the woods. Pass through a gate and follow the path slightly left to a stile and gate at the edge of the wood.

❷ Follow the stony track to the steps. At the top, turn left. Look for a signpost on the left of the track. It points towards a ladder stile. To go to the falls turn left and return to continue the walk. Further up the valley the path divides.

❸ Take the lower path, on the left. The path ends but carry on to a very straight and deep stream bed. On the far side is a wire fence. Turn left, downhill to where the stream joins the main stream. Go downstream to where the water is shallower. Cross, turn right and make for the corner where the two fences meet.

❹ Cross the gate and turn left. Go to the left of the sheep pens and then turn right, following a little stream uphill until you can cross it. At the conifer trees, cross the gate and follow the fence on your left. At the top of this first rise there are good views of the Berwyns.

❺ Keep going with the fence on your left. The track eventually rises to the highest point of the walk. It then drops again and takes a sharp turn left in the first of a series of bends into the valley on your left. At the bend leave the track, using sheep tracks to reach a path alongside a fence below you. Aim for the rowan tree. Now turn left and follow the path along the fence. Pass a stile on your right and you will come to another one leading into a wood.

❻ Follow the path through woodland and some small clearings until you see some fencing on the right below you. You will soon come back to the iron bridge. Cross it to get back to the gate.

The remote peaks of the Berwyns are wild and deserted, populated only by grazing mountain sheep.

As well as a magnificent waterfall, this footpath offers the walker superb mountain views.

④ **③**

Afon Disynfa

P C

Pistyll
Llanrhaeadr

Tan y Pistyll

②

①

B4396

⑥

⑤

Craig y Mwn

access information

The easiest access to the falls is from the A483 just south of Oswestry. Turn off at the White Lion on to the A495. Turn right on the B4396 to Llanrhaeadr-yn-Mochnant. A well-signposted, but rather tight right turn in the village leads to a narrow road with passing places. The falls are along this road. There is some roadside parking, but parking at the café, an old farm, is inexpensive.

0		1 km	1 mile

▲ Map: Explorer 265
▲ Distance: 4 km/2½ miles
▲ Walk ID: 1567 Jim Grindle

Difficulty rating

Time

▲ Lake/Loch, Toilets, Museum, Church, Good for Wheelchairs, Café, Food Shop, Good for Kids, Nature Trail, Restaurant, Woodland, Ancient Monument.

St Winefride's Well from Holywell

This walk in Greenfield Heritage Park includes St Winefride's Well, one of the Seven Wonders of Wales. There is one main track running through the park. Smaller paths lead to the old railway and industrial sites.

1 From the car park take the signposted path towards the Visitor Centre. Just before you reach the centre there is a path going off to the right. Follow this path. On the right there is a garden on the site of the Abbey Wire Mill. Continue on the path to the left until you reach a reservoir.

2 Take the fork to the right so that you keep by the edge of the water. A little further on the path divides. Take the right fork and stay on the path until you have to go up left to the railway track. The railway track is the level path on the right. Stay on this until you see some gravelled steps going down to the right.

3 Take the little path down the steps and stay on it until you have to go up left to the railway. Take the right branch, which is the old railway track. Look for a flight of steps going up to the left, but ignore them to stay on the track. Watch now for a split in this track.

4 Take the right fork at a red and white marker post 8JF. Just out of sight is a small gate by a larger one. Go through the small gate and drop down through an industrial area to the B5121. You will see a footpath sign on the left of the opening on to the road. Turn left.

5 About 100 m up the road is the entrance to St Winefride's Well. After visiting the famous well, go back the

way you came and stay on the old railway track. This will bring you right back to Basingwerk Abbey, passing by features you have passed earlier. The track takes you over a little bridge and then it curves down to the left to the ruins of the abbey.

6 Go through the little gate to the abbey. At the far end is a similar gate. The car park is also signposted.

further information

Wheelchairs can be used for this walk by omitting the sections with steps – all the paths join up again on the old railway.

The estuaries of North Wales can provide some of the most spectacular views in Britain.

Holywell lies between the A55 Expressway and the A548; both Basingwerk Abbey and St Winefride's Well are signposted. Buses from Chester to Rhyl call at Holywell. The car park on the B5121 is closest to the Visitor Centre, but the car park on the A548 for the abbey can also be used.

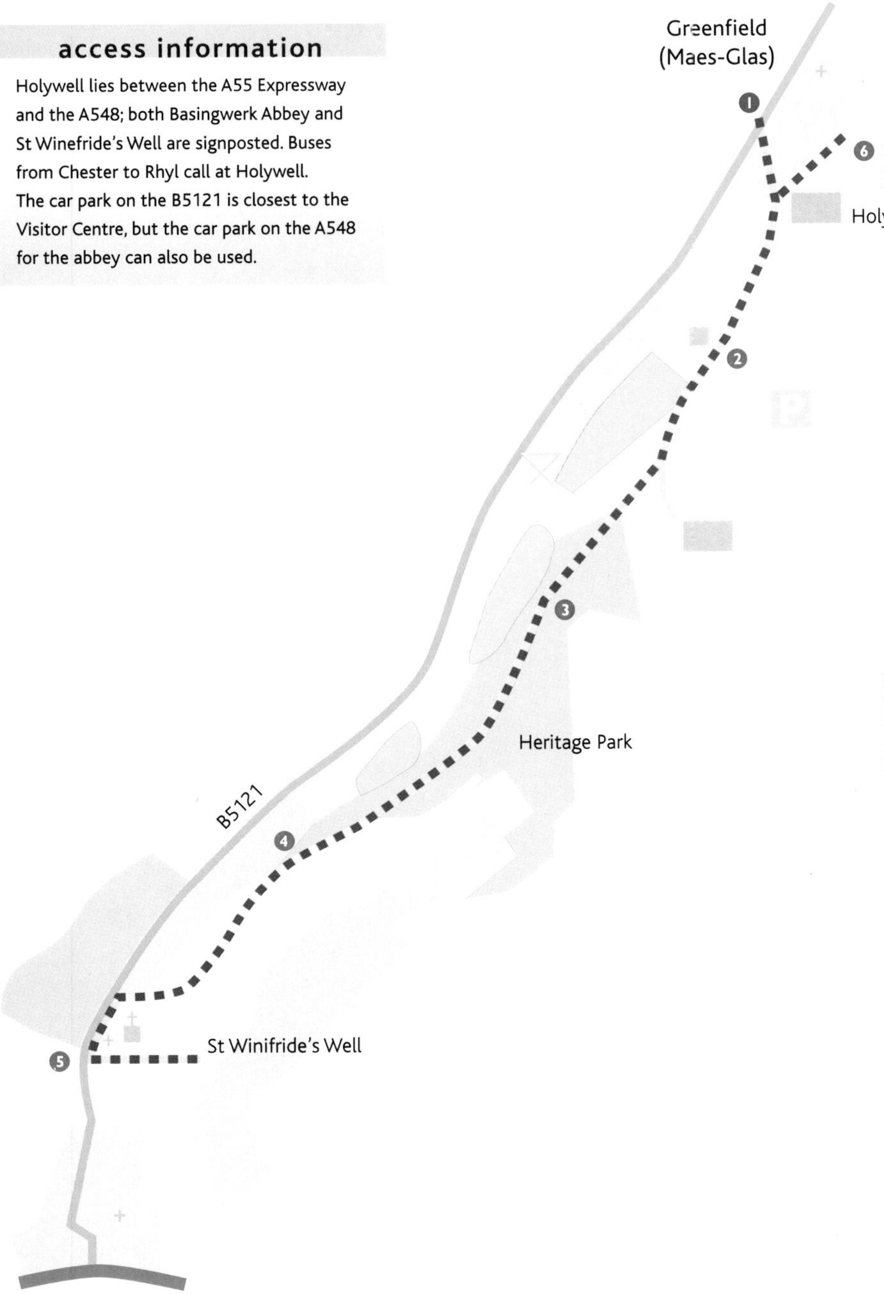

Greenfield
(Maes-Glas)

Basingwerk
Abbey

Holywell Visitor Centre

Heritage Park

B5121

St Winifride's Well

The monks at Basingwerk Abbey were the first to harness the power of the nearby stream.

0   1 km   1 mile

▲ Map: Explorer OL 14

▲ Distance: 5 km/3 miles

▲ Walk ID: 213 Peter Salenieks

Difficulty rating

Time

▲ River, Pub, Toilets, Church, Wildlife, Birds, Great Views, Cafe, Gift Shop, Tea Shop, Woodland

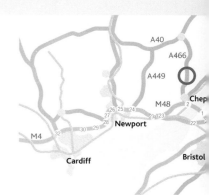

Devil's Pulpit from Tintern Abbey

This is a short walk from the atmospheric, ivy-clad ruins of Tintern Abbey along woodland paths that lead to the Devil's Pulpit, overlooking the Wye Valley. The route follows part of the Offa's Dyke Path.

❶ From the car park opposite Tintern Abbey, walk along a minor road that leads towards the River Wye. Pass the Anchor pub to reach a footpath on the left. Follow the footpath along the bank of the river. After the footpath turns towards Tintern, pass a whitewashed house on the left and continue along a minor road to reach a T-junction with the A466.

❷ Turn right and continue along the pavement, passing a hotel on your left and an art gallery on your right. Continue until you reach a minor road junction on your right, just past the Abbey Mill.

❸ Walk along the minor road towards the River Wye and cross the footbridge. Continue along the footpath, passing another footpath on the right. Follow the path on the left as it leads uphill, with several metal posts at the start. Shortly after it levels off, there is a junction. Take the right-hand path and follow it until you reach another junction marked by a wooden post with a footpath sign.

❹ Take the right-hand path. At the next junction, turn left and follow the footpath uphill. As the gradient levels off, the path bears to the right. Climb the short flight of wooden steps on the left to reach a junction marked by a wooden post with a footpath sign.

❺ Turn right and walk along the track. At the next junction bear left and follow the footpath uphill to reach Offa's Dyke Path. Turn right at the footpath sign and walk along Offa's Dyke Path until you reach a junction and a sign at a right-hand bend.

❻ Continue along Offa's Dyke Path from the footpath sign to reach the Devil's Pulpit. Retrace your route to the start.

The Devil's Pulpit juts out from the cliffs beside Offa's Dyke, high above the River Wye.

access information

Tintern lies between Monmouth and Chepstow in the Wye Valley. The abbey is just off the A466, at the southern end of the village. There is a car park just off the main road. If this is full, the car park for Tintern Abbey is at the rear of the abbey, beside the River Wye.

further information

• This walk can be combined with a visit to Tintern Abbey. Contact the information centre on 01291 689251 for information about when the abbey is open.

• The Devil's Pulpit is a small limestone rock that juts out from the cliffs. It looks down over Tintern Abbey from the hills beside Offa's Dyke on the eastern side of the River Wye. Local legend has it that the Devil stood upon the Devil's Pulpit to preach to the monks below, tempting them to desert their order.

The view of Tintern Abbey from the Devil's Pulpit takes in a vast expanse of the River Wye.

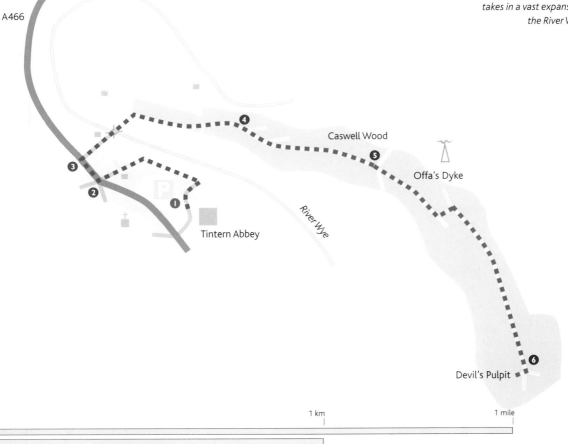

A466

Caswell Wood

Offa's Dyke

River Wye

Tintern Abbey

Devil's Pulpit

0   1 km   1 mile

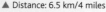

▲ Map: Explorer 152
▲ Distance: 6.5 km/4 miles
▲ Walk ID: 999 John Thorn

Difficulty rating

Time

●●●●◗

▲ Pub, Castle, Birds, Flowers, Great
Views, Butterflies, Industrial
Archaeology, Public Transport,
Woodland, Ancient Monument

Ruperra Castle from Draethen

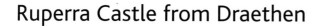

This is a pleasant walk that follows a route almost entirely through varied woodland, with the added interest of passing the ruins of Ruperra Castle and an Iron Age fort along the way.

❶ From the centre of the village walk up the road signposted Rudry and Lisvane. At the bridle path sign, turn right up a concrete drive. At the cottage, turn left to follow the bridleway sign, through a gate, then another gate into the woods. Just after the track levels out turn right at a T-junction, then left. Emerge onto an open area with several paths.

❷ Take the gravel track slightly to the left. Almost immediately take a hard-to-see path that drops down steeply to the left. Towards the bottom of the valley, where the path turns right and the woods open out a little, turn left past a ruined cottage. Cross the road by going left then right down a drive marked 'The Retreat'. Go between the houses. Do not turn left into a gate, but cross a gravelled area, go down some steps and cross a footbridge. Take the left-hand path up through the woods. Cross a track and continue. Pass a steel barn on your left, go through the gate and turn left onto a road. Just past a cottage, bear right, keeping the woods on the left and the field on the right.

❸ At the end of the field, go through the kissing gate and follow the wall, crossing two stiles. At the end of the wall, turn left to a gateway for a view of Ruperra Castle. Retrace your steps back to the wall, then turn right past the gateway marked 'Ruperra Castle Farm'.

Bear left, slightly uphill, for another view of the castle.

❹ Before you reach a gateway, turn left uphill following yellow arrows. When you reach another path, turn right to climb the ridge to the top of the Iron Age hill fort. When the track turns sharp right, follow it down, then left.

❺ Turn right at a junction then right at the next junction to return to point 4. Climb away from the wall but continue across the next path, following the arrows. Turn right at a wider track.

❻ Turn left onto a narrow path. Continue down through the woodland. Go through a kissing gate into a field. Follow the right-hand side of the field down into the valley. Turn right at the stile to reach the starting point.

The original 17th-century castle of Ruperra was twice destroyed by fire and was rebuilt once. It is now nothing more than a romantic ruin.

Ruperra Castle was built to command views across a swathe of countryside.

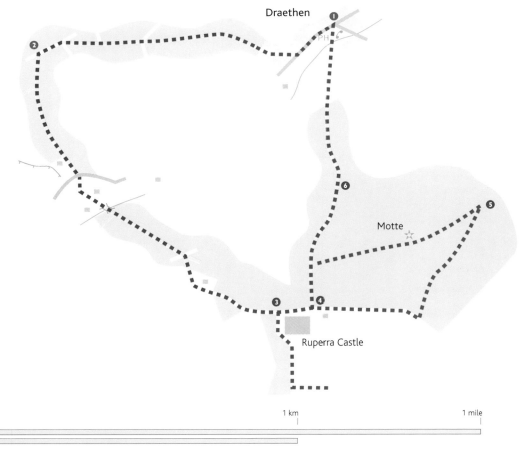

▲ Map: Explorer OL 35
▲ Distance: 11 km/6¾ miles
▲ Walk ID: 1323 Pat Roberts

Difficulty rating

Time

▲ Mountains, Wildlife, Birds, Flowers, Great Views, Butterflies, Moor, Tea Shop, Woodland

Carningli from Sychbant

This walk climbs to Bedd Morris, then onto Carningli, for incredible views of the Wicklow Hills in Ireland, the Welsh coast and the Preseli Hills, to return down through the Gwaun Valley.

❶ From the car park walk up the drive to Ffald-y-Brenin (Sychbant on the map). Where the drive swings left, go over the marked stile to the left of the gate. Continue up a field to pass through another gate. Turn left to reach a gate with blue arrows. Go through the gate and turn right up a green lane. Go over two stiles in quick succession to enter the forest. An information board tells us that this is the 'Penlan Project'. Follow the arrow to the right, to Carningli. After about 1 km bear left towards Bedd Morris and emerge from the forest on a stony track.

❷ At Bedd Morris, with the stone behind you, walk ahead on a path that follows a raised bank in an easterly direction, leaving the bank to curve slightly left over the top of Mynydd Caregog. After passing above the forest, a fence comes in from the right. Follow the grassy path, keeping the fence on your right. As you come level with Carn Edward, a large rocky outcrop on the right, take the left fork, then turn immediately left again.

❸ Keep heading towards Carningli, following any of the small paths. Once you are within 150 m of the outcrop, head for the northern end, and you will see a well-used route up onto the top.

❹ At the top of Carningli there are fantastic views. Retrace your steps off the outcrop, and turn right. Take the

most suitable path round the rocks. Descend on the narrow but good path heading east. Follow the path down to the Dolrannog road.

❺ On reaching the road turn right. Go through the farmyard and walk through a metal gate to pass Dolrannog Uchaf.

❻ At the end of the road go through the gate to the left of the bungalow. Follow the bridle path down through the woods to reach Llanerch and the valley road. Turn right to return to the start.

further information

There are many legends attached to Bedd Morris, but it is most likely a Bronze Age standing stone and is now one of the markers standing on Newport Parish Boundary.

An ancient copper beech tree presides over the Preseli Hills like a monument to the enduring power of nature.

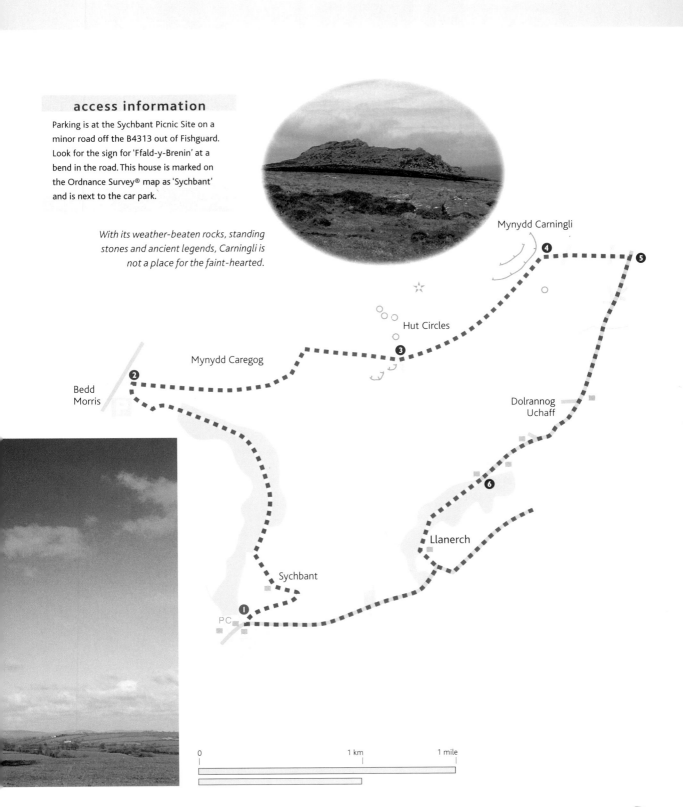

access information

Parking is at the Sychbant Picnic Site on a minor road off the B4313 out of Fishguard. Look for the sign for 'Ffald-y-Brenin' at a bend in the road. This house is marked on the Ordnance Survey® map as 'Sychbant' and is next to the car park.

With its weather-beaten rocks, standing stones and ancient legends, Carningli is not a place for the faint-hearted.

Mynydd Carningli

Hut Circles

Mynydd Caregog

Bedd Morris

Dolrannog Uchaff

Llanerch

Sychbant

PC

0   1 km   1 mile

▲ Map: Explorer 200
▲ Distance: 9 km/5½ miles
▲ Walk ID: 951 Pete Brett

Difficulty rating

Time

▲ Hills or Fells, Reservoir, Toilets, Play Area, Church, Wildlife, Birds, Flowers, Great Views, Good for Wheelchairs, Nature Trail, Tea Shop, Woodland

Garreg-ddu Reservoir from Elan Valley

This relatively short walk offers the walker peace and tranquillity amidst superb scenery.

1 Leave the car park taking the ascending path to a cinder track and turn left towards Caban Coch Dam. Remain on the track beside the reservoir until reaching the arched road bridge.

2 Cross the road by Foel Tower and rejoin the track. (If time permits you can turn left over the road bridge and visit Nantgwyllt Church on the far bank.) Leave the track through the gate and continue on the grass verge beside the road for 200 m to the bridle path on the right. Climb the bridle path steeply at first then over the stream, ignoring any small side tracks.

3 Where the path branches left, continue straight ahead towards high ground for all-round views. From the viewpoint return to this point and descend the path, following small posts and signs to reach a metal gate.

4 At the gate turn right and continue to descend, following little yellow markers until you reach a wire fence. Turn left and follow the fence to the gates of the water treatment buildings. Go through the gates and down steps to the road.

further information

Wheelchair users can follow the route alongside the reservoirs, returning to the visitor centre the same way.

5 Cross the road. Behind the houses, cross the footbridge over the river. Turn right and follow the river through the Elan estate to pass the toilets on the left. Go through a white gate beside the bridges into Cnwch woods and continue on the path through the trees.

6 Go behind the first turbine house and cross the bridge in front of the dam. Head behind the second turbine house to return to the visitor centre car park.

The bridge over the majestic Caban Coch Dam forms an integral part of this walk.

access information

From Rhayadar take the B4518 road heading south-west (follow signs to Elan Valley Reservoirs) and park at the Elan Valley Visitor Centre.

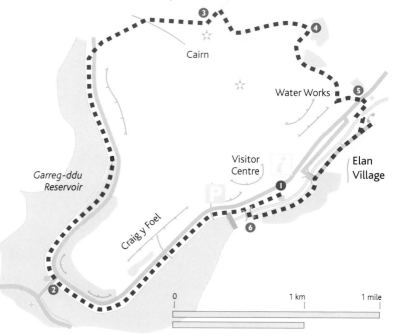

▲ Map: Explorer OL 12
▲ Distance: 11 km/6¾ miles
▲ Walk ID: 1290 John Thorn

Difficulty rating

Time
●●●●

▲ Mountains, Reservoir, National Trust, Wildlife, Birds, Flowers, Great Views

Brecon Beacons Horseshoe

This walk to the top of the Brecon Beacons has stupendous views from almost every point.

❶ Do not go through the gate but turn up to the right to reach a track. Cross the stile and walk between the two fences. When the fence on your right turns right follow it up. As you approach the trees bear left to join the rough track. Turn left onto the Roman road. Go down a steep dip and up the other side, bearing right. Follow the track to the top of the pass.

❷ At the top, cross the stile on your left and bear left on the well-defined path that climbs around the shoulder of Cribyn. At the saddle between Cribyn and Pen y Fan, continue ahead climbing steeply. Look over your right shoulder for views of Cribyn, Llangorse Lake, the Black Mountains and, later, the Sugar Loaf.

❸ The summit of Pen y Fan has commanding views in all directions. Descend towards the flat top of Corn Du, but at the saddle bear left. At the next saddle bear left again, climbing slightly to follow the escarpment for about 3 km. You pass to the left of a large cairn, following the edge. Pass another large cairn and ignore the steep path down to your left in a fold in the mountain.

❹ Turn right to start a steep descent, aiming for the end of the dam. Go though the gate, walk along the dam then veer off to the right to cross a bridge. Go through the gate to reach the starting point.

access information

Start at the parking area by the dam of the lower Neuadd reservoir. Access is from the minor road between Vaynor/Merthyr and Talybont off the A465.

The Brecon Beacons.

further information

Pen y Fan (see photo on page 58) is the highest point in South Wales. Do not attempt this walk in poor visibility. Most of the paths on the first part are well defined but less so after leaving Corn Du, and parts of the route can be muddy or boggy.

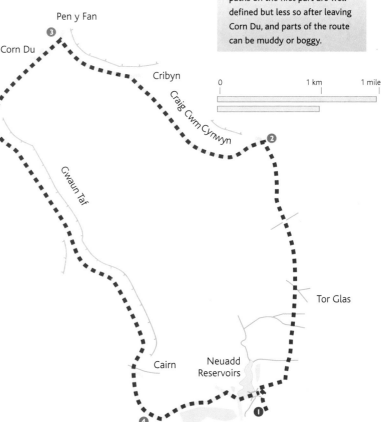

▲ Map: Explorer OL 13
▲ Distance: 10 km/6¼ miles
▲ Walk ID: 1511 Pat Roberts

Difficulty rating
👣👣👣

Time
●●●◖

▲ Mountains, Pub, Wildlife, Birds, Great Views, Industrial Archaeology, Ancient Monument

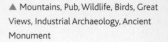

Blaenavon from Foxhunter Car Park

This walk in the Blaenavon heritage area takes in a visit to the Ironworks, as well as views of Big Pit and Coity Mountain. The return route is across opencast landscape, past old mines with fine views of the Brecon Beacons and the Black Mountains.

❶ From the car park walk to the minor road by the masts and go right for a short distance. Take the narrow path on the left towards the telegraph poles. Just above a covered reservoir join a gravel path to reach the B4246. Turn left towards Blaenavon. As you reach the 30 mph signs, cross the road.

❷ Opposite the Riflemans Arms, take a path through a car park and picnic area, to emerge on a road. Cross over to reach the footpath and head downhill. Soon take a right turn, just after a left bend, where you can see the ironworks on the right. Just after the bend, go down the steps in front of York House. Cross over to join another road with the ironworks railings on your right. Continue down the road to visit the ironworks.

❸ Head down the hill and take the first turn on the right. Follow this road to join the B4248 road to Brynmawr. Turn left and continue until you reach a bus shelter on your right.

❹ Just past the bus shelter, take the lane up towards two houses. Where the lane swings right, continue ahead on a track. Go over another stepped gate and through another gate to follow the track up into the open hillside.

❺ You will come across a square chimney stack with a tree growing out of the top. To each side you will see fenced-off areas. Continue on the track

to reach another fenced square. Ignore a yellow arrow pointing straight on and head for the incline on the right.

❻ At the ridge there are views of Brecon Beacons and the Black Mountains. Take the right-hand path towards the masts. Maintain direction, heading just right of the masts, until you reach the B4246. You should emerge opposite the side road leading to the masts and car park.

access information

Park at the Foxhunter car park, near the masts on the Blorenge. Take the B4246 road from Abergavenny to Blaenavon, and turn off near the Keeper's Pond at the top, heading for the two big masts. These should also help you to navigate the walk.

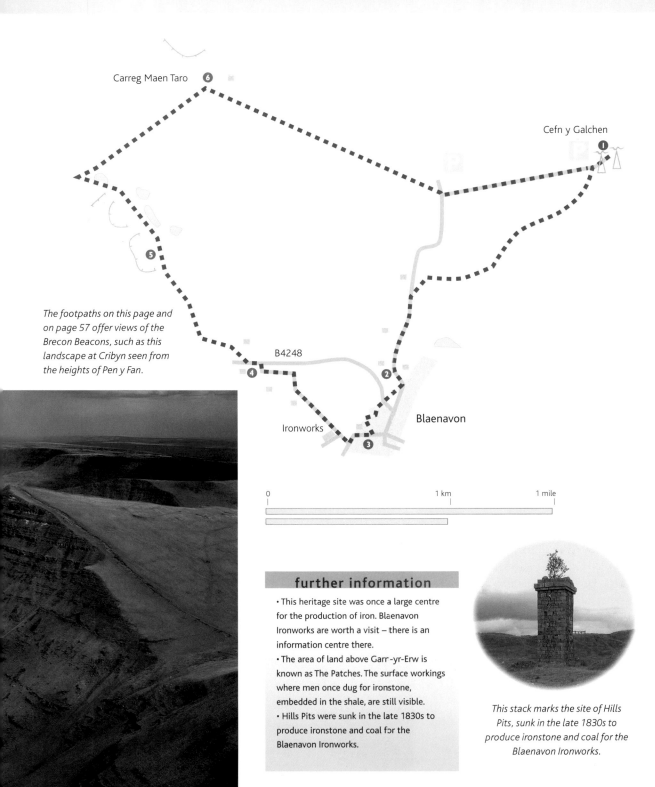

Carreg Maen Taro ❻

Cefn y Galchen ❶

❺

❹

B4248

❷

Ironworks

❸

Blaenavon

The footpaths on this page and on page 57 offer views of the Brecon Beacons, such as this landscape at Cribyn seen from the heights of Pen y Fan.

0   1 km   1 mile

further information

• This heritage site was once a large centre for the production of iron. Blaenavon Ironworks are worth a visit – there is an information centre there.

• The area of land above Garr-yr-Erw is known as The Patches. The surface workings where men once dug for ironstone, embedded in the shale, are still visible.

• Hills Pits were sunk in the late 1830s to produce ironstone and coal for the Blaenavon Ironworks.

This stack marks the site of Hills Pits, sunk in the late 1830s to produce ironstone and coal for the Blaenavon Ironworks.

▲ Map: Explorer OL 13
▲ Distance: 13 km/8 miles
▲ Walk ID: 1270 Pat Roberts

Difficulty rating

Time

▲ Mountains, Church, Wildlife, Birds, Flowers, Great Views, Butterflies, Waterfall

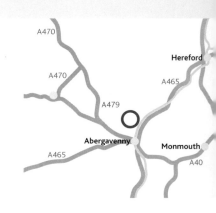

Revenge Stone from Pont Esgob

This route combines two ridge walks with a visit to an attractive old church, a memorial stone with a very unusual name, an Iron Age hill fort and a walk in the Grwyne Valley.

❶ Take the minor road signed Partrishow and Crickhowell. Keep right at the fork and follow the road, ignoring the road on the left. Just below the church, approach the Holy Well of St Issui by paving stones on the right.
❷ Walk through the churchyard and through a gate onto the hillside. Join a track, and, above the farmhouse on the right, head right and down, keeping the wall on your left. Pass between the buildings to reach a track. Go through the first gate on the left and cross a field to a stile. Continue down the next field to a stile and then left and down past ruins to reach another stile by the road.
❸ Cross the road and continue down the minor road. Pass the chapel and keep to the road. Keep to the right of the farm and buildings and keep to the main track leading gently upwards. At the farm, keep to the right of the farmhouse to reach a gate, which leads to a sunken stony path. Continue through another gate, keeping to the right wall. As the wall swings right, go straight up to the ridge and the memorial stone.
❹ At Dial Garreg (The Revenge Stone), turn right to walk the ridge. At the fork, take the left path to reach a wide, grassy track, heading towards Twyn y Gaer. As the wall and track start to swing away from the fort, and there is a junction of

paths, continue on the central green track up to the top of Twyn y Gaer.
❺ Retrace your steps down from the top and at a cross paths fork left, keeping to the fence on your left. Cross the stile and head down, across grass and then on an old drovers' road between two old walls.
❻ At a break in the wall, keep to the right of the wall to reach a stile onto another stony track. Continue bearing left and down to join a road, then right and down, eventually to reach the starting point of the walk.

further information

• The Revenge Stone marks the spot where the Norman Marcher Lord, Richard de Clare, was attacked and killed by Morgan ap Owen in 1135.
• Twyn y Gaer is a fine Iron Age fort with extensive views.

Seen here from a point near Crickhowell, Powys, the Black Mountains provide a majestic background to the landscape.

No public transport. Parking is at
the roadside, at Five-ways, Pont
Esgob. This is on a minor road
between Lower Cwmyoy and
Forest Coal Pit, off the A465 just
north-east of Abergavenny.

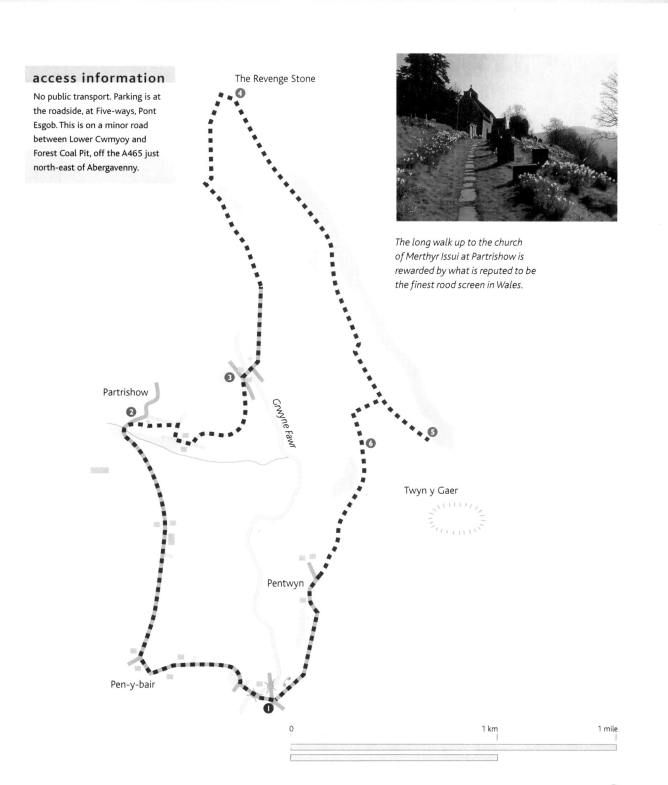

The Revenge Stone

Partrishow

Grwyne Fawr

Twyn y Gaer

Pentwyn

Pen-y-bair

0   1 km   1 mile

*The long walk up to the church
of Merthyr Issui at Partrishow is
rewarded by what is reputed to be
the finest rood screen in Wales.*

▲ Map: Explorer OL 13
▲ Distance: 8 km/5 miles
▲ Walk ID: 307 Peter Salenieks

Difficulty rating

👣👣

Time

● ● ●

▲ Hills or Fells, Mountains, Pub, Toilets, Church, Great Views

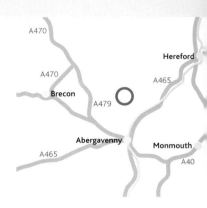

Hatterrall Hill from Llanthony Priory

This is a short circular walk set in the heart of the Black Mountains, with fine views of the surrounding hills and plains. At the start or end of your walk, you can wander among the Gothic arches of the ruined Llanthony Priory.

❶ As you leave the car park walk straight ahead, keeping the Abbey Hotel and Llanthony Priory on your right. A short distance ahead, there is a footpath sign next to a gate and a stile. Cross the stile and turn right. Keep the Abbey Hotel on your right and walk for about 100 m.

❷ Cross the stile and follow the sign to Offa's Dyke. The footpath leads along a track across a field. Close to a small stream, turn left at the National Park marker and walk a few metres to cross the first of a series of five stiles. The path leads gently uphill across fields towards Loxidge Tump. There is a National Park sign next to the fifth stile, which includes a map of Hatterrall Hill. Now the path climbs through bracken, before bearing right and zigzagging to gain the ridge. Cross open ground along a path, which passes a small cairn before joining Offa's Dyke Path at a milestone (signed Llanthony).

❸ Turn right at the milestone and walk along Offa's Dyke Path for about 3 km. The path dips into a col, where another milestone points to Longtown and Llanthony.

❹ Turn right and follow the footpath down towards Llanthony, taking in the views of the Vale of Ewyas. Continue for about 1.5 km along this footpath until you reach a junction with a footpath

sign and a stile on the left, together with a National Park sign.

❺ Cross the stile and follow the footpath downhill, keeping the fence on your left. Cross another stile and enter Wiral Wood. The footpath bears right then left at a small stream, before crossing another stile at the edge of the woods. Cross the field to a stile in the bottom right corner.

❻ Cross the stile and follow the dry-stone wall, keeping Llanthony Priory to your left, until you reach the stile at point 2. Cross the stile and retrace your route to the start.

access information

Approach the start by road from Abergavenny or Hereford along the A465 to Llanvihangel Crucorney. Then follow minor roads for 10 km to reach Llanthony. Park in the free car park at Llanthony Priory.

Abandoned by the Augustinian monks in 1134, Llanthony Priory's ruined skeleton stands forlornly in the shadow of the Black Mountains.

further information

Pony trekking can be arranged at Court Farm, which is immediately adjacent to the Abbey Hotel.

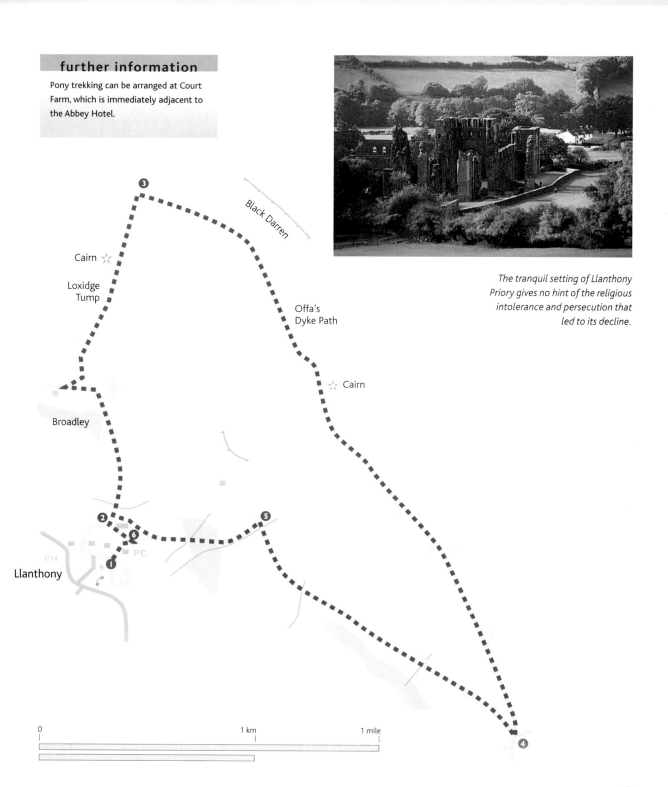

The tranquil setting of Llanthony Priory gives no hint of the religious intolerance and persecution that led to its decline.

Black Darren

3

Cairn ☆

Loxidge Tump

Offa's Dyke Path

☆ Cairn

Broadley

2

6

PH

PC

1

Llanthony

5

4

0   1 km   1 mile

Index

acknowledgements

The publishers wish to thank the following for the use of pictures
CORBIS: pps. 8/9 Eye Ubiquitous, 10/11 John Heseltine, 12 Eric Crichton, 15 John Noble, 17 John Heseltine, 18 Derek Croucher, 30 Wildcountry, 31 Michael Busselle, 32 Robert Estall, 38 Eric Crichton, 40 John Heseltine, 43 AlanTowers/Ecoscene, 48 Adam Woolfit, 54/5 Chinch Gryniewicz, 56 Peter Hulme, 58/9 Andrew Brown/Ecoscene, 60 Derek Coucher
JIM GRINDLE: pps. 14, 36, 46, 47, 49
HUTCHISON PICTURE LIBRARY: pps. 20/1 Bernard Gerard, 62 Robert Francis
PAT ROBERTS: pps. 29, 33, 55, 59
NICHOLAS RUDD JONES: pps. 26/7
PETER SALENIEKS: pps. 28, 50/1, 63
JOHN THORN: pps. 22/3, 24/5, 34/5, 52/3, 57